BUILDING Beyond THE 9 to 5

INSPIRATIONAL LESSONS from **SUCCESSFUL BLACK WOMEN**

edited by **KIOSHANA LACOUNT-BURRELL**

Building Beyond the 9 to 5: Inspirational Lessons from Successful Black Women

Copyright 2021
All Rights Reserved

Published by Thrifty Mama Media, LLC (Gadsden, AL)

No portion of this book may be reproduced, scanned, sold, or distributed in any form, whether printed or electronic, without the express written consent of the author(s).

Editing and typesetting by: Kioshana LaCount Burrell

Cover design by: Julian Long

First Edition, September 2021

ISBN: 9798465327800

DISCLAIMERS AND LEGAL NOTICES:

The information presented herein represents the view of the author(s) as of the date of publication. Because of the rate with which conditions change, the author(s) reserve the right to alter and update their opinions based on the new conditions.

This book is for informational purposes only. While every attempt has been made to verify the information provided in this book, neither the publisher nor the author(s) assume any responsibility for errors, inaccuracies or omissions. Any slights of people or organizations are unintentional.

If advice concerning legal or related matters is needed, the services of a fully qualified professional should be sought. This book is not intended for use as a source of legal or accounting advice. You should be aware of any laws which govern business transactions or other business practices in your country and state.

Any reference to any person or business whether living or dead is purely coincidental.

Dedication

For all the women out there chasing something beyond the ordinary - this is for you.

We believe in you, and we are cheering for you.

Table of Contents

Foreword: Never Stop Hustling

Shevvy Malibu   9

Determine Your Path

Chapter One: Work Your WOP – Planning for Strategic Success

Sheena Morgan   15

Chapter Two: That One Time God Called

Ristina Gooden   23

Chapter Three: Doing Too Much… And Loving It

Lishala Carter   32

Chapter Four: Creating Your Unique Lane

Qiana Martin   39

Chapter Five: Daydreaming About My Destiny

Keita Pyfrom   48

Develop Your Plan

Chapter Six: Building the Foundation for Entrepreneurial Success
Kioshana LaCount Burrell — 57

Chapter Seven: The Art of Failing
Veronica Marz — 67

Chapter Eight: The Season of Success
Marci Bryant, MBA — 74

Chapter Nine: Becoming… Ms. Corporate-preneur
Porche' Maloney — 89

Chapter Ten: Level Up Your Leadership –Becoming a Career Competent and Confident Leader
Cassie Catrice — 98

Dictate Your Terms

Chapter Eleven: Finding Balance and Establishing Boundaries – A Recipe for Success
Alysha M. Campbell — 110

Chapter Twelve: Building Up and Breaking Through – Overcoming Setbacks and Positioning Myself for Success
Jessica Canty   119

Chapter Thirteen: Winning from Within
Dee Burrowes   132

Chapter Fourteen: Wearing Two Hats - Transparency and Authenticity as an Employed Entrepreneur
Sydney Davis   142

Chapter Fifteen: Strategy, Balance, and Staying the Course
Christon Stewart   150

Define Your Legacy

Chapter Sixteen: Crafting My Table
Katrina Caldwell   159

Chapter Seventeen: A Legacy Built on Love
Deon Hall-Garriques   171

Chapter Eighteen: Breaking Cycles, Building Legacies
Akiba Canady   182

Chapter Nineteen: Mastering Freedom

Jessica Cammack   194

Chapter Twenty: Preparing for the Harvest

Kiki Lazz-Onyenobi   202

Acknowledgements   209

Foreword: Never Stop Hustling
Shevvy Malibu

I have this problem with the word "never".

It's not the problem most people would think. I don't say things like "never say never," or admonish others who say they'll "never" do something again... I say never all the time. And when I say never, I mean it. For better or worse, my never has always been absolute. That's my problem.

So when I tell you I NEVER thought I'd be an entrepreneur, understand how much I mean **_never_**.

I realize it might feel more inspired to say I've known since I was a little girl that I wanted to run my own business, but the truth be known, when my 4th grade teacher asked me what my dream job would be, I told her I'd be grow up to a ballerina or the Godfather of a major crime family (these are still aspirations). I may not have had entrepreneurial aspirations, but what I knew even then was that I wanted to live my life on my terms and – I NEVER wanted a regular job.

Life has a funny way of laughing at how I use the word "never". I held quite a few regular jobs as I got older. Now, I never _wanted_ any of them - but I took them. I had kids who had developed this nasty habit of eating every day (sometimes three or more times!) and food and clothes were (surprisingly) not free. The local crime families were all staffed up, and by 25 – the way my knees were set up – ballet wasn't a viable career choice. I took regular jobs to stay insured and help care for my kids. I knew I wanted something beyond that, but I didn't exactly know what that was.

The one thing I knew for sure was that I **never** wanted to be an entrepreneur. I'm not even really sure why - my family is full of women doing the damn thing. When I was a kid my mother had her own hair salon, then later she became a private accountant. After that she bought a restaurant and then a grocery store. When I was in my teens, my aunt owned and operated a bakery. Later in her life, my grandmother parlayed a love of fine furnishings into an interior design consultancy. Today, both my sisters have businesses. Sunni runs an art and design studio and is a traveling tattoo artist, while Semone runs the family restaurant and does corporate and private gifting. Somewhere along the way, despite my misgivings about entrepreneurship, I looked up and found myself being the founder and marquee host of Bossy Media, the publisher of BOSSY! Magazine, and the owner/proprietor of English-Brown, a winery I run with my (serial entrepreneur) mother. I say all the time that I don't know how I got here, running all these businesses, but when I look at all the Black women around me doing it and making it work – I don't know how I thought I could avoid it.

My dream job might have changed a bit (I didn't become a crime boss – I became BOSSY! Instead), but my desire to live a life on my own terms never has. Now more and more Black women are making this choice every day. And that's what entrepreneurship is - at the core of it – it's the choices you make every day.

It starts with choosing to put a little more time into that side hustle, or choosing to research how to do something yourself instead of paying a premium for someone else to do it. You choose to put yourself out there and let other people know what you can do. You start choosing to charge for your work because you're worth it. Then you choose to invest a little more back in – little more time, a little more capital. One day you realize that the choices you've made start making choices for you. Those little steps move you to step out a little further. For me, if I ever had to make one big choice to go into business for myself or just stay put, I never would have chosen entrepreneurship. Yet somehow, every day I kept choosing myself and eventually those little choices became my business. As Black women we owe it to ourselves to choose ourselves. And when you choose yourself don't ever let anybody question that choice – that's **your** business.

When I first started BOSSY! Magazine, I spent a lot of time searching for every day Black women bosses doing great things in their industries, in an effort to recognize their contributions, and I hoped to inspire others to do the same. These days we are everywhere and I'm so here for it. This is our season. We are being encouraged – NO – **called** to explore our passions, follow our dreams and FINALLY get the coins we deserve. From side hustles and passive income streams to online empires or full-fledged brick and mortar establishments, the faces behind our new favorite brands look like us and it doesn't get more BOSSY! than that.

This book is the collective dream of 20 great Black women who took those first shaky steps and kept on walking. It is a reminder that every single one of us who follows a passion and chases down that dream until we catch it is doing something great. The inspiration to look beyond what you know and build something better doesn't have to come from larger than life moguls like Oprah, Rihanna, or Beyoncé. The real inspiration often comes from the voices nearest to us. Our sisters, our aunts, our mothers, our friends – all of them tired of working harder and being compensated less than our counterparts have driven us to create new streams of income.

There's NEVER going to be a better time.

You'll NEVER regret choosing yourself.

Once you see what's possible you'll NEVER want to look back.

And when I say NEVER – I mean it.

Never stop hustling.

Shevvy Malibu

Former dancer and model Shavon Brown (aka Shevvy Malibu) has a knack for wearing many hats. This serial entrepreneur has a proven track record of corporate excellence that took her from executive assistant to CEO. She has written for numerous media outlets such as CBS, AXS.com, and The Examiner and chronicled her unique view on life, love, and family in her blog "I Just Want to Be Superwoman."

As a host, she conquered radio as co-host on the hilarious Reality & Relationship show and the live show area as the moderator of Heavesdrop. Inspired by her own mother's entrepreneurial efforts, this wife and mother of four founded Boss Moms, a networking enterprise that supports women entrepreneurs in balancing family and business. She has taken another step towards building a media empire as Editor-in-Chief of BOSSY! Magazine and the Creator and host of BOSSY! Live Weekly Radio show, A certified life coach and public speaking coach, Shavon strives to reach even more women and help them grow.

Connect with Shevvy:

Instagram: https://www.instagram.com/getbossymag/
Facebook: https://www.facebook.com/getbossymag
Email: editor@getbossymag.com
Website: http://www.getbossymag.com/

Determine Your Path

Sheena Morgan

For more than 20 years, Sheena has helped minority, and women-owned businesses realize develop strategic plans and strategies that support healthy and solvent growth.

Before launching, Lengo Strategic Partners, LLC, she managed the certification of over 50,000 applicants as Executive Director of the South-Central Texas Regional Certification Agency and the North Central Texas Regional Certification Agency. She oversaw the supplier diversity program for Atmos Energy moving on to Manager Public Affairs for Southeast Dallas Region.

Connect with Sheena:

Email: sheena@lengofocus.com
Website: https://www.lengofocus.com
LinkedIn: https://www.linkedin.com/in/sheenadmorgan
Instagram: https://www.instagram.com/lengofocus
Facebook: https://www.facebook.com/lengofocus

Chapter One:
Work Your WOP - Planning for Strategic Success

Sheena Morgan

Niche': The specialized segment of the market for a particular type of service or product.

Niche': Commonly referred to as a noun and adjective is a word that pivots the trajectory of your business.

In business, the concept of understanding your niche is of critical importance. If you aren't "niched-down" enough, you will fail to connect to your desired target audience and ineffectively position your marketing. If you are unsure of your "niche market," you will have difficulty determining how to provide a solution. We often think about finding our niche in familiar and comfortable markets with people we know and trust. In doing this, we often fail to understand what problem we are attempting to solve and if that "niched group" is affected.

So, how do you find your niche? Well, if you ask 10 people, you will get 10 different answers. I started my work in the supplier diversity and minority business certification programming industry in 1999. I had no idea then that I would be sitting here now as a corporate professional and entrepreneur, and if I had, I know I would have paid closer attention to the signs and opportunities that I clearly missed! At the beginning of my career, I had the chance to develop close relationships with business owners seeking minority certifications and learn some intimate details related to business ownership, trials and triumphs. I would spend the next 20 years developing frameworks and methods to help bridge the gap between the business owners and resources to leverage assets and build healthier and more viable business models.

I didn't realize that my passion for the minority and woman business owner would cultivate a desire to step beyond the confines of a professional career and launch the first iteration of my business **Lengo** in 2016. Did you catch that "first iteration"? When I opened my business, my niche markets were start-up minority and women-owned businesses. The mission of Lengo then was to develop competitive advantage business plans that would help owners understand their market placement and prepare them for scalable growth. Most of my clients were in the ideation stage of business development and sought out the fundamental elements of starting a venture. My niche was derived directly from the network of an industry that I was familiar with.

In 2020, like many of us, I found so much time to really work on my business and position it to meet an entirely different need within the B2B minority and women-owned business market. I decided to formally organize with the State of Texas and re-launched Lengo Strategic Partners, LLC, focusing on maximizing workflow optimization and improving organizational and project performance. My niche is called Simone/Simon 3.0. They are my ideal client and are composed of the elements and indicators that comprise my niche market. Simone or Simon 3.0 are the owners or presidents of an organization with at least 50 employees and annual gross revenue of $2.5M or more. They are entrepreneurs and serve the B2B markets in heavy highway construction and professional services.

Now, let me tell you, it was not easy to trim the fat and get to the substantive meat of my niche because I struggled with the thought of the anticipated future opportunities that could come my way and would have to be passed up. After all, they were outside of my scope. This is the moment you must STOP and understand that you have no control over future opportunities. Furthermore, trying to be everything to everyone will not drive the success of your venture. I had to consider what would be best to grow my business and how to do that with a singular solution.

So, let me ask you a question. Are you working within or outside of your WOP? WOP stands for **Window Opportunity Plan Strategy**. The WOP Strategy was developed to help my clients identify growing markets, streamline processes through clarified differentiation strategies, and shift the culture from risk-averse efforts of constant competitor-based marketing, leading to decreased profits and dysfunction processes. This was the method I used to clearly define my niche market and audience.

You see, the task of finding your niche shouldn't always be dependent on a current marketplace. Many successful businesses have created uncontested market space and new demand by innovating products and delivery methods. Additionally, they focused on their differentiating factors and not hedging out the competition. I want to leave you with a different approach to niching that has helped me tremendously.

The WOP is composed of a **Window** (who), **Opportunity** (what), and a **Plan** (how).

Ask yourself the following questions first:

1. Who is your current client?
2. Who are your competitors?
3. What resources are you lacking?
4. What resources do you have at your immediate disposal?
5. Why isn't your current strategy working?

Then I want you to ask yourself:

1. Who could you target today with your current resources?
2. Would you be the only one in this space?
3. What is your differentiator?
4. Is there market demand for your solution?
5. What are the infrastructure or process alignments needed?

Next, identify the **Window** or the new industry you want to target. For example, I desired to remain close to minority and women entrepreneurs, but I needed to refine the vertical. So, I decided to focus on B2B clients within the entrepreneurial space.

Then, identify the **Opportunity** or the success factors within the Window. Keeping with my example, I had to consider what areas of their business operations my solutions would be most beneficial and analyze the optimal success position. With the impacts of COVID-19 and workflow optimization, organizational processes, and project communication pathways being significant factors in business success, that is where I chose to align my solution.

Finally, design the **Plan** or the process to support this new targeted Opportunity. Consider the infrastructure, assets, capital, staff, and process realignments needed to deliver your solution to this new targeted group.

Success is birthed from calculated risks. Suppose you are operating in a saturated market space and trading your value for cost instead of pricing the solution's value based on beneficial outcomes. In that case, you are not niched, nor are you operating in an environment conducive to sustained scale or growth. It was a leap of faith for me to transition from a commonplace to one that required me to focus on one thing for one particular subset of clients. But in doing so, I was able to create solutions that are valuable to my clients.

The journey to entrepreneurship is not easy, especially if you are still working a regular job as well. Not only are you trying to navigate how to divide your time, energy, and money to birth your dream or help it grow but, you are also juggling life. During my re-launch plan, I was diagnosed with breast cancer. I was 39 and had a son in college, a mortgage, a career that I enjoyed, and now an intruder on everything that I knew to be normal. I had a threat to my existence living in my breasts, and I didn't have a clue what to do and how it would end up. I had long talks with God and realized I had to focus on what was happening to me right now. So, my business went dormant for one year. I wrapped up the last two clients, buckled down, took time off my job, and focused on my health, family, and life. It is incredible what can be revealed or become so clear when the distractions that we often call necessities are not there anymore. I spent my days journaling, planning, and thinking. I came out of 2019 renewed and refreshed, unsure where the future was taking me but excited for the ride. I unpacked trauma and started tearing down the walls of fear and uncertainty and honoring the elements of my being that made me evermore enough and never too much.

As they say, I stepped out on faith. I decided to stop perpetuating what I thought people would think and care more about how people experienced me, challenging myself to show my more authentic, connected, vulnerable self and becoming willing to be seen in all my brilliance. As a Black Queen, I know the value that I bring to the table; I am aware of the frequencies of my vibrations and that not everyone will vibrate with me. A niche is more than a business term used to define your marketplace or audience. Your niche is comprised of every element of your being. Beyond my business, my life work must recalibrate to ensure I am not competing in a space that fails to bring value to others or myself. I am constantly identifying opportunities to help others that I hadn't thought of before and, most importantly, planning ways to support my ability to be of good service to myself, my family, friends, and complete strangers.

I take this energy and intention with me now through everything I do. There is a quote that I will leave you with. I begin my proposal meetings with this reminder to myself and a mindset shift for potential clients:

> **"You must celebrate the milestones as you prepare for the road ahead." – Nelson Mandela.**

Ristina Gooden

Ristina Gooden's work centers on her belief that what is central to God's love for God's people is that we all flourish. She exercises this belief through her writing, preaching, and speaking on topics about faith, race, gender and sexuality, and pop culture through a womanist lens.

A licensed minister in the Baptist Church tradition, Ristina is a third year student at Vanderbilt Divinity School, concentrating on Religion, Gender, and Sexuality. She also serves as president of the Vanderbilt Divinity School Black Seminarians.

Originally from Cleveland Ohio, Ristina holds a Bachelor of Science degree in Hospitality Management from The Ohio State University. She has seven years of experience as an event planner, having worked at OSU and Spelman College.

Connect with Ristina:

Instagram: https://www.instagram.com/womanist_baker/
LinkedIn: https://www.linkedin.com/in/ristinagooden/

Read more about Ristina's journey here:

Wall Street Journal: College Was Supposed to Close the Wealth Gap for Black Americans. The Opposite Happened. (wsj.com)
Medium: I Cook, I Clean, and I Still Don't Have a Ring | by Ristina Gooden | Medium

Chapter Two: That One Time God Called...
Ristina Gooden

Dear Ristina,

Congratulations! On behalf of Dean Emilie Townes and Vanderbilt Graduate and Professional Admissions, I am pleased to share that you have been accepted into the Master of Divinity program for Fall 2019...

***

It was 8:30 AM on Saturday, April 13, 2019. I had just awakened in my Atlanta apartment where I had only been living for 8 months. I had moved to Atlanta as an opportunity to try something new. I had previously been living in Columbus, Ohio for 10 years – including four years as an undergraduate at The Ohio State University and an additional six years as a working professional at the institution. I felt like I had seen and done everything I needed to in Columbus in that time. I had planned well over 4,000 events, escorted celebrities through dingy back hallways and loud kitchens, run through security to catch 6 AM flights to meet the best and brightest of Buckeye Nation, eaten cold gourmet dinners out of event to-go boxes on the floor of my rarely enjoyed apartment, sleepily driven home after midnight only to be back in the office at 7 AM, and asked, more times than I cared to count, if someone had actually registered for *this* event.

Don't get me wrong. I loved being embedded into the fiber of what made my alma mater so great. It truly is a magical place.

I just... needed a change.

I traded my scarlet and gray t-shirts of Ohio State for a pristine white dress (with a few hints of Columbia blue), and made my way in a new role at Spelman College.

At that point, I thought I had made it. Moving to "Black Hollywood" surely meant I would soar in my career, meet the love of my life, and finally begin to truly live. Except... I didn't. The first day I sat down at my desk at Spelman I realized I didn't want to be an event planner anymore. I could feel the joy and passion I once had suddenly drain from my body. All I could think about was the thousands of dollars I had just shelled out to move, the ten-hour journey from Columbus to Atlanta with my best friend, the boxes - so many damn boxes, and the world I said goodbye to just a week prior. What in the world was I going to do now?

You Have Been Accepted.

I never imagined going to graduate school. I loved school dearly but could never settle on what I actually wanted to be when I grew up. I had applied to undergraduate with plans of becoming an anesthesiologist. Once accepted I switched to international business and then food science before finally settling on hospitality management. I remember my parents being furious at first but they finally came around once they realized my job prospects were quite promising. A degree isn't necessarily required to be an event planner so a graduate degree would have been completely useless. I had tried taking classes in graphic design but could not keep up with the class work while clocking consistent 10 hour days in my "day" job. I toyed with the idea of going to culinary school, a childhood dream of mine, but could not wrap my mind around the cost of attendance versus the projected salary. So I chose to be content with the education I already had.

Then, one day in January of 2019, I found myself in the midst of a conversation with my dear friend and now mentor, Mashaun, about his experience in seminary. As we spoke, I found myself becoming more and more intrigued. I was enthralled by this idea of wrestling with who God is and finding ways to address social justice issues through the lens of the church. I didn't even know seminaries existed, let alone ever thought about applying to one. Yet, as soon as he walked away from my desk that morning, I immediately started exploring this newfound concept.

Union Theological Seminary...
Vanderbilt Divinity School...
Princeton Theological Seminary...
Yale Divinity School...
Candler Theological Seminary...

On Behalf of Dean Emilie Townes...

I honestly had no idea what I thought I was doing. I hadn't been in church in 10 years. I had no religious training or experience outside of occasionally doing the announcements at church or being the mistress of ceremonies for Youth Day back in 2003. Growing up, folks often said I was called to ministry, but my phone must have been turned off because I never got that message. I grew up in a strict, conservative, religious household, but now at 29, I found I wanted nothing to do with church. Yet for some reason, it made sense at that moment to pursue this – something inside me was pushing me to look further into this idea instead of leaning away. As I browsed through the programs and faculty, I was simply blown away. Vanderbilt had a Black lesbian woman as its Dean and more Black faculty than I had ever experienced or thought to expect. Union Theological is often touted as the hub of progressive theology and is the former (and now future) institution of Cornel West. That was intriguing enough for me.

So, I made a deal with God, as we often do when we want to do something, but are hesitant. We do this, of course, because it allows us to blame God if things don't quite work out the way we hope. I like to think of this as the human way of hedging our bets – we are free to pursue whatever it is that we want to do, but don't necessarily have to bear the full brunt of rejection if things don't pan out the way we imagine. My deal with God went something like this: I would apply to two schools, Union and Vanderbilt. If by some miracle I got accepted and received some scholarship money, I would go. If not, I would continue on my search for fulfillment (or at least, contentment) in my professional life and put to rest these abiding thoughts of seminary school.

To me, it sounded like an impossible deal. Here I was, seven years out of undergrad and working a full-time job. I hadn't written a paper, let alone three essays, since graduation! There was simply no way anyone was going to let me into their school. I hit submit on my application to Vanderbilt on Tuesday, April 9, and went on about my day, fully convinced that this would be the end of that particular dream.

Congratulations!

Four days later, however, God took the opportunity to show me just who God is. They came through on their end of the deal, in a major way. Not only was I admitted, but I also received a substantial scholarship. Staring at my acceptance letter in quiet disbelief, I called my parents and delivered my news. My dad laughed for two minutes straight because he was in shock. How could his daughter, the one who only showed up to church to socialize, be accepted into divinity school and actually consider going? I, too, was baffled.

I called my best friends - they were in shock as well, but we took a shot to celebrate anyway.

I texted Mashaun - he was proud and supportive and that has not changed.

Just a few weeks later, I was asked to preach a sermon for the first time. God was really showing out now, but I should have known that this was only the beginning. I have now just begun my third and final year of divinity school. In this time I have served as President for both the Student Government Association and the Black Seminarians, received two fellowships, preached my trial sermon and become a licensed minister. I continue to work as a program coordinator at Faith Matters Network, a womanist-led organization committed to pursuing and facilitating positive social change. All of this is on top of meeting the most kind-hearted, justice-focused humans this world has ever seen.

The focus of my degree is Religion, Gender, and Sexuality and I am doing work around sexual liberation for Black women. That comes from my own experience of growing up in purity culture - a hot topic in the religious world that seemingly only applies to female-identified bodies. I am on a quest to rid us of this toxic ideology so that we can fully embrace our sexuality. It's a battle I fully intend to continue fighting both in the pulpit and the world.

I do not see this experience through rose-colored glasses. Saying goodbye to a job that paid nearly $60,000 a year with full benefits was hard. Moving into a studio apartment from a two-bedroom apartment was hard. Adjusting to being a full-time graduate student that had to write papers and take tests was hard. Adding to my student loan debt was hard. Diving headfirst into a completely different field of study and career at nearly 30 was hard. It all continues to be difficult to navigate through, especially with the addition of a global pandemic. Yet, through it all, I'm confident in knowing that it has all been worth it.

I finally feel like I am where I am supposed to be. Opportunities have been presented to me that I could have never imagined. I guess folks were right all along - I was called to do this work. It may not look like they imagined (Folks often think I spend my days reading the Bible, singing hymns, and talking about Jesus. If you replace the Bible with womanist theology and hymns with the latest Cardi B song then you'd be a lot closer to right). I do find myself talking about Jesus quite a bit, but not in the way many think. I like to remind folks that Jesus was a Black man and refugee. He hung out with sex workers and flipped tables in the temple. His first miracle was turning water into wine at a wedding. Jesus sounds like my kind of guy, but He doesn't need to be everyone's guy. Choose whoever you want, just seek to do justice, love mercy, and walk humbly with your chosen Divine being. Amen? Amen.

If I could offer a few words of advice for anyone else who may be trying to figure out if there is something *more* out there for them beyond whatever job they're doing now, it would be that if something piques your curiosity, follow that trail until you can decide if it is something you want to take a leap of faith for. There are many things that I love that I have followed a trail for, only to realize it needed to stay a passion and not become a paycheck. Others, like my career change, have worked out beautifully. I would not have known either if I didn't try. Finding out what that *more* is does not always have to completely disrupt your life. I had the privilege of not being tethered to a partner, child, or family that relied upon my physical presence or financial contributions. If you also have that luxury, JUMP! And enjoy the journey. If that is not the case for you, start smaller by taking a class, volunteering, reading, talking to people in the field, or just following people on social media. Then keep taking small steps in the direction you want to go and see where that leads you. We only get this life in this body one time, so it would be a disservice to yourself if you didn't chase at least one wild dream.

As I look towards the future, it looks like I'll be making another deal with God this fall, this time for a Ph.D. in homiletics or rhetoric. Homiletics is the art of preaching or writing sermons. Rhetoric is what I call the "secular" version of homiletics. There are very few Black women who get their Ph.D. in Homiletics since women are rarely given the opportunity to preach (so why would we get an advance degree in it?). I hope to become a public theologian that works at the intersection of race, faith, sexuality, and pop culture. I hope to find ways to redefine what we deem as sacred and how that can show up in our preaching. In short, how can the lyrics of Cardi B, Lizzo, or Jazmine Sullivan be considered revered and a source of liberation. I hope to leave behind a legacy that allows for us to see the sacred in all things, not just scripture. This is the work my soul must have, as Rev. Dr. Katie G. Cannon would say.

I have my snacks ready for the journey.

Lishala Carter

Lishala is a native of Gadsden, Alabama where she currently resides with her husband, DeAngelo and children, London, Landry and DeAngelo, II. She currently works for United Way as the Program Director of 211 First Call for Help. She has a BS in Criminal Psychology, MA in Public Health, she is also a Certified Doula, Childbirth Educator, Master Herbalist and published author (Reigning While It's Raining). She is also serving as the Toys for Tots Coordinator for Etowah County and a proud member of Delta Sigma Theta, Inc.

She is the founder and executor of Time Wise Consulting, LLC a company that focuses on progression and business organization. Lishala is also a partner in a new adventure, VisitHer, LLC which focuses on holistic Healthcare and wellness through non-traditional medicinal methods. Lishala has been known to host empowerment events for women to encourage presentation of best self with no limitations. Amongst all these hats she loves family time and crafting and she also loves writing.

Connect with Lishala:

LinkedIn: https://www.linkedin.com/in/lishala-thomas
Facebook: https://www.facebook.com/Visither
Website: www.VisitHerWellness.com
Website: www.TheLishalaBrand.com

Chapter Three: Doing "Too Much"... and Loving It
Lishala Carter

Picture it... A breastfeeding baby boy, a tumbling, "Momma, look at me!" six-year-old, a Tik-Toking, YouTubing middle schooler, and an entrepreneurial, "Hey, what about this idea?" husband... and then there's me. The milk master. The audience. The purpose-pushing, secretarial, agenda setting woman of the house. I wear many hats for my family – but there's more to me than my commitments. Beyond the needs and wants of my loved ones, I also have an extensive list of things that I enjoy and am committed to, for me. I am traditionally employed in a 9-5 setting, a Certified Doula and Childbirth Educator, a consultant (Time Wise Consulting), a published author (Reigning While It's Raining), an active member of Delta Sigma Theta Sorority Inc., a founding member of Purpose Pushers, and Partner/Co-Owner of VisitHer, LLC. - and these are just the things that I am primarily involved in! I am a philanthropist at heart, and I find that much of my life is dedicated to the progression and advocacy of those around me. It isn't difficult to see why I'm often told that I'm "doing too much" – but I love it.

I have learned over the years that what looks like too much to someone else may be just that, too much (for them). My plate may look full from the outside looking in, but the truth is, as far as I'm concerned, I do not have a plate – I have a platter! I walk forward with the confidence of knowing that I am built to carry my portion, no matter how heavy it may seem to other people. There are seasons when the heaviness does feel overwhelming. However, I understand that the heaviness is not due to "doing too much", but is instead caused by imbalance and an inability to effectively communicate my needs, ask for assistance, or to delegate. Ouch!

Often as women, more specifically as Black Women we find it easier to assume all the responsibilities rather than express how we need and/or desire assistance. Over the years I have come to accept that the "do it all" mentality is also a method of avoidance and in some instances a defense mechanism. We avoid involving others as a means of avoiding conflict, insufficiency, fear of failure, lack of commitment, or complicating relationships. I recall as a young girl witnessing my grandmother work hard at church programs, family reunion planning, and countless outreach opportunities. She would sit at her dining room table and plan for hours. She would simultaneously cook a meal, plan a reunion for over 500, and help us with homework - but never would she ask for help. I admired the strength, the ability, and the willingness without realizing the deficit in this method. The older I got and the more she shared, I gained understanding as to why she worked the way she did, persevering, independently. Black culture in life lessons is learning, doing, being, what we witness – whether deliberately or inadvertently. I have learned that this method of working, doing all, being all is one of those inadvertent inherited behaviors.

Learned behaviors are difficult to undo sometimes. We find that we value traits and behaviors learned without hesitation. It is with time and personal experiences that some of the misguided, but unintentional flaws become learning and refocusing points. While strength to do is admirable, we want to learn strength in the HOW TO DO IT! It is not the weight that makes it impossible. It is the posture with which we carry the weight that determines the possibility!

We must correctly identify our why for "doing too much" and determine if it's because we really love it, or because we don't trust others enough to help us in our journey. I mentioned that my day job consists of the traditional in office time commitment. I also mentioned that when that "doing too much" becomes heavy it is necessary to evaluate balance and delegation. It has taken me 32 years to truly learn what balance really is. I admit that I have possessed most of my life what I now know is a false sense of balance. As a creative and entrepreneur, I have struggled with turning off and not allowing the "doing too much" to do too much. I have struggled with rest, effective vision casting, effective goal setting and a host of other areas due to my misunderstanding of balance. In my earlier grasp of the concept, I thought that balance was taking on everything without complaint, simply crossing things off my to-do list. Boy was I wrong! After failures, hearing no repeatedly, and ultimately slamming into multiple brick walls, I took the time to delve into how I could better serve myself, my family, my purpose, and my creativity. I learned the importance of delegation, rest, and purpose. These three areas of realization have helped me become better in many areas of my life.

Purposed involvement is not tiring when it is done from a place of certainty and self-awareness. Purpose is the valve that connects the heart to motion. Purpose is why your stomach feels butterflies, your palms sweat, you lose sleep sometimes, and you fiercely carry on! Understanding purpose is crucial in being able to do all that we do. By nature we were created with wombs, which means that whether a mother or not we have the ability to nurture and bring forth whatever we desire. We have the responsibility to protect our creative space (womb). We best impact those around us by nurturing purpose and birthing from this place with confidence and assertiveness. Being cognizant of how our purpose impacts our creativity is paramount for success. As a creative entrepreneur I have learned the importance of what is purposed for me to facilitate and what I am simply exposed to for the purpose of collaboration or advisement. Differentiating between ownership and advisement was and still is difficult because remember I can easily "do too much" and love it! This is when understanding your purpose is essential.

Understanding your purpose will help determine what and how to delegate. This was and still is a difficult task for me sometimes. Often times as women, more specifically Black Women we find it easier to assume all the responsibilities - rather than express how we need and/or desire assistance. The inability to delegate exposes an inability to trust wholly. As a Black Woman I have learned in the world of entrepreneurship that trusting is sometimes harder than actually starting a new endeavor. I have come to learn the value in delegation. It has helped me overcome many hurdles in projects. Being able to delegate has afforded me better time management, fostered relationships and built amazing collaborations. Delegation has also increased my ability to build simultaneously. Creativity does not allow us to be closed minded and in most cases it eliminates the "one man band" approach to projects, which yields room for delegation and trust. In the "doing too much" it is healthy to garner trusting, reliable relationships. A successful entrepreneur understands the importance of impactful collaborations and communications through delegation.

Communication is healthy and allows room for so much growth and even rest. As a "do too much" person, I have to be mindful of the status of my physical and mental health at all times. Rest is essential to my continued effectiveness. I do love "doing too much" with appropriate balance and understanding when to rest. Rest is healing and fuels the mind to stay strong and capable. It is a beautiful thing when the body possesses the power to heal itself through a reset, rest. Creative entrepreneurs often struggle with the need to rest. We find it hard to turn our brains off. It can sometimes feel like we are looking for permission to take the needed rest. I have been guilty in the past of not feeling like I deserve rest. I had to experience a paradigm shift as it relates to rest. When I allowed myself to not just rest but to enjoy rest, I felt better, I thought better, I produced better. Challenge yourself to rest more. Rest for me is not always sleep. Sometimes rest for me is walking barefoot in the grass, underneath the sun with no responsibility or agenda. Other times it is a nap so good that I awake with lines embedded on my face as proof that I entered into REM sleep. Determine what your rest looks like and commit to enter into it when you know you need it.

The need to "do too much" isn't a bad thing and no one should convince you otherwise. You know what your cup can hold. You know what makes your heart beat fast with great anticipation and not dread. Being an entrepreneur is about freedom of expression. Allow yourself to invest in your freedom no matter what it looks like to anyone else. Your plate is catered to your palette. You owe it to you to establish a life that you love living! Remember to discover purpose, trust delegation, and enjoy rest relentlessly! After all, it is your "too much" to do!

Qiana Martin

Qiana Martin, MSA is an Accountant from Detroit, MI with more than 10 years of experience in Accounts Payable, Receivable and lease accounting for various companies.

Qiana currently works as an Accountant for Georgia Tech and owns Q Faces, LLC where she does face and body painting along with henna, glitter tattoos and the occasional balloon twist here or there.

Connect with Qiana:

LinkedIn: https://www.linkedin.com/in/qiana-martin-ba-msa-353b4418/
Facebook: www.facebook.com/facepaintingbyqfaces
Instagram: https://www.instagram.com/qfaces/
TikTok: https://www.tiktok.com/@q_faces?lang=en
Website: www.QFaces.com

Chapter Four: Creating Your Unique Lane
Qiana Martin

I often get funny looks when I tell others that I am accountant by day and a face painter on the weekends. Interesting mix right? It certainly isn't the path that I ever saw myself taking – in fact, growing up, I actually had aspirations of becoming a lawyer. I made it a point to include my dreams of becoming an attorney in my life plan, even pursuing multiple after school programs with lawyers in high school. When I went away to college, however, I quickly realized I actually hated criminal justice as a major. I also didn't think I could stomach a career as a lawyer after learning more about what it entailed. The truth is, it just wasn't in me.

Instead, I discovered that what I was really interested in was business. I loved the business courses I was taking in undergrad and had enjoyed them in high school as well. Because of this, I made the decision to switch majors, letting go of my litigation dreams and pursuing a career in accounting instead. Even then, I knew I wasn't your average run-of-the-mill accountant. Though I didn't realize the talent I had inside of me until years later, I pursued and flourished in my accounting career. It was a great foundational move for me.

Before I graduated with my BA in Accounting, I worked for one of the Big 3 automotive companies. At the young age of 20, I was working in a plant thinking I could pay for school that way. I worked in positions that it took others years to get into. I don't think I was lucky - I was extremely blessed. I worked there for almost seven years before I took a buy-out and returned to my studies to become an accountant. This job, however, is where I found my gift. Every summer, we would have an annual family picnic sponsored by our union. Each year the union would ask for volunteers to help make the event successful. One year I checked the list, saw face painting and thought that would be a fun thing to learn how to do. I love kids and knew it would be helpful at our event.

After arriving and checking in for my first day of face painting duties, I was given one small brush, eight primary colors and a book of images. I was told, "There's water on the table!" with a smile, and then immediately thrown into the deep end. I asked if there was some type of training, and the response I received was, "Do the best you can….." Needless to say, I was shook! Now what am I supposed to do? I was second guessing all my decisions at that point and was considering asking if one of the food servers wanted to trade with me.

Instead, I decided to woman up and walked over to the area for face painting, buckling down for an interesting day. There were three others at the face painting station, and they'd all been given the same instructions I was. Although I was a bit nervous, I settled in for a fun day at the office picnic and gave it my best shot.

Much to my surprise, the day went amazingly well! In fact, it was such a success that I was requested to do it again the next year, and for all the following years until I left to return to college. Once I made the transition out of that job, I didn't touch a brush again for years. Though this had been a fun little venture, it wasn't something that was a big deal in the context of my life and career up to this point. In fact, I didn't even think about face painting again as I went on to complete my undergraduate degree and gave birth to my child.

Then one day, several years later, I came across an old paint kit and began practicing on myself and my son who was around 4 at the time. I found that I had really missed the creativity afforded to me by this little hobby and continued doing my little "gig" for family, birthdays, and random fun days with my son for the next three years. At some point, I decided that I'd like to become a professional face painting artist. I found that it didn't matter how long it had been since I picked up a brush, it was always natural when I did again.

Face Painting by Qiana was born in 2015 in Michigan. In just four short years I went from answering a Craigslist ad for a little girl's super hero birthday party to growing and developing what is now a bustling and burgeoning small business (That little girl, by the way, has grown into an amazing young woman that I follow by way of her parents on social media). In 2019, I decided to relocate to Georgia, prompting me to begin my small business again in a whole new state. So far things are going well. My business is gaining momentum as I leverage the power of social media to generate leads and allow me to book gigs on a basis that becomes more and more consistent with each passing day. Although this is a new start for me, I am confident in my ability to succeed and I look forward to my progress!

Fourteen years on from my first experience touching a paint brush, creativity continues to come naturally to me. That does not mean that I don't continue to study and practice in order to grow and improve. So often we take our natural talents for granted and fail to properly nurture them. Anything worth having takes hard work and dedication. I love joining competitions to challenge my skill. My most recent was a butterfly challenge. Each day for two full weeks, I was challenged to create a new and innovative design. Every morning I was given a daily theme, with instructions to produce an original piece by the end of the day. Out of 14 days, only four were on the weekend, so I made sure I carved out time to expand myself. Because I am a busy mom who is balancing both a business and my day job, time management is a critical component of my overall success.

When an idea comes, I have to write it down, sketch it, save an inspirational image, something to keep that mojo fresh. I get so excited when I pick up a brush and learn a new stroke.

My heart literally smiles every single time a child squeals with delight over the design I gave them. It stokes their imaginations and their own creativity. There is something about a child thinking up a character on the spot and asking for it. It brings out my own creativity as my adrenaline pumps and I tap into my connection to this little person I just met. This talent evokes empathy and helps me be more than just a face painter. By the end of most encounters, I've become instant family with my clients. I have lost count of how many events I have left with babies now dubbing me their "Auntie". Children meeting me years later have told me they remember the butterfly or tiger I painted on their faces long ago. I believe everyone has a talent deep inside them. The one that comes to you in the blink of an eye and will leave you just as fast if you don't acknowledge it. It took me so long to see mine for what it was. Don't wait too long to find your niche and develop it.

    Face painting is more than what many think it is. While it is a field that is very creative and artsy, you don't necessarily have to be Picasso to be good at it. In my case, I cannot draw well at all! My family recently learned that the hard way choosing me to play Pictionary thinking they had the golden ticket. They did not – in fact, we nearly lost because they were depending on my (nonexistent) drawing skills! While I'm no sketching expert, I thoroughly enjoy the freedom and creativity that comes to me when I paint. I am a whimsical artist. I love swirls and curls, glittery, girly stuff. I also enjoy skulls and sugar skulls, having developed this particular affinity after learning more about the Day of the Dead (Día de los Muertos) holiday native to Latinx culture.

I also enjoy the freedom that comes with building your own enterprise. As I said earlier, my business is currently in the rebuilding stage. I have had to virtually start over from step one since relocating. However, because I have an established following back home in Michigan, I know what I am capable of building the same thing here in Georgia. The more that I paint and post my work, the more it is seen. The law of attraction is working its magic in the Peach State and I am getting more calls and referrals for events. I am encouraged for my future! When you own a business, you have to speak positivity over it at all times just as you should speak positivity over yourself and your life daily. In the future, I would like to teach others how to face paint and launch a business in this field. Specifically, I would love to work with teenagers who have an interest in art. We never know how far we can go in life when someone sees greatness in you.

For me, finding my way in the corporate world did not come as easy as my business did. I started my undergraduate thinking I would become a lawyer and ended with an accounting degree and a newborn child. My strategy throughout college was simple: I dug deep and paid attention to the classes I enjoyed as well as the classes I excelled in during high school. I loved all of my business classes and especially enjoyed my accounting and finance classes. With that in mind, I eventually switched gears and my major to match. Mine was not the traditional route at all – in fact, it took 12 years to get my bachelor's in accounting. When I finally graduated at 30 years old, I did so as a new mother with a 4-month-old baby in my arms. Still, I was and am thankful that through God and sheer determination, I made it to the finish line! I was the first grandchild in my family to graduate from college and again the first to graduate with my master's degree a few years later.

    I also learned a lot about myself along the way. Before I even finished my bachelor's degree, I knew that I would not be your typical CPA-type of accountant. I am way too silly and whimsical to stay as serious as an IRS accountant or investigator. My graduate studies took me in the direction of business and project management, developing the hybrid skills that help me in my day to day living and work all the time. Pursuing my Master's degree took yet another six years to complete, however. I spent many years trying to get my foot in the door with my education and work experience. It took moving to another state for everything to come full circle and for my journey to finally all make sense. I have such a sense of peace where I am now. I know the sky is the limit now.

    I tell you these stories to say that I don't think I completely chose this life. It very much so chose me. My why in all of this is my family, especially my son. I wanted to show him it is never too late to pursue a dream. It is imperative that you nurture your talents. You have to practice and improve. There will always be an opportunity to learn and grow. I found my niche in this world simply being myself. I love face painting and enjoy the smiles that I receive from each happy client. While my business feeds my creative talents, I also love that accounting enables me to dig into my intellectual side. Although it drives me nuts when I am investigating why an account is off by a few dollars or where a payment needs to be applied, I have a huge sense of accomplishment and satisfaction when I find the problem. I describe myself as an "Artistic Accountant" - I get to be an original in the midst of so many.

Both my 9-5 and my 5-9 help me help others. I find myself being a counselor in both areas. It comes naturally to put others at ease in my presence. My desire and love of helping others makes working as both an accountant and as an artist fulfilling. I encourage others reading this to pursue the same in their own lives and careers. Find things that make you happy. Find things that don't always feel like work. That is what will most likely be your thing. Your skill or hidden talent may very well be your forever calling! Don't ignore your talents. Don't ignore your desires. They all work together seamlessly for your best. Make sure you never stop learning and becoming a better version of yourself. Keep feeding your mind and your soul until you find your way, then go some more!

Keita Pyfrom

LaKeita Pyfrom, known to personal and business friends as Keita P, is a Creative Enthusiast, Mother, Mental Health Advocate, Community Servant, Serial Entrepreneur, and Founder of Detroit Balloon Bar. Keita is driven by innovative thinking combined with passion to serve her community by leveraging multilayered skill sets. She works to spread awareness about anxiety and depression by speaking about her own experiences. As an expert in her field, Kieta teaches others to tap into their skill sets and provides guidance to an efficient work/life balance.

A single mother of two entrepreneurial sons, Keita loves to spend time with family and explore life as it is served up each day. Her vision is to Be transparent while exploring options of using creativity as a guide to fight anxiety, depression, and other forms of mental health illness as an entrepreneur.

Connect with Keita:

LinkedIn: https://www.linkedin.com/in/keita-pyfrom-7a7b67ab/
Facebook: https://www.facebook.com/detroitballoonbar
Instagram: https://www.instagram.com/detroitballoonbar/
Website: https://www.detroitballoonbarexpress.co/

Chapter Five: Daydreaming About My Destiny
Keita Pyfrom

Daydreaming in La-La Land

Remember as kids, people asked us the question, "If you could be anything in the world, what would you be?" For me, the answer to that was never a simple one. I wanted to do everything! While most of the time this thought was only when I was daydreaming, it allowed me to step outside of my conscious life and imagine the possibilities surrounding me. Imagine sitting at your table sipping your favorite drink and all of a sudden you get stuck in this trance of staring off into space. You're awake, but you feel detached from reality. Suddenly you're living out a scenario that only you can see in your mind – but it feels real. If you're a creative type like me, you probably find yourself doing this a lot. For most of my life, I've found myself daydreaming regularly, living out my ideal life in my head. Unfortunately, though most of the time those daydreams never translate into real life.

Finding Myself

When I graduated from high school, I really didn't have anyone to mentor and drive me in any specific direction. I just knew I wanted to make money, so I enrolled at my local community college in a computer program. Before I completed my Associate's degree, I dropped out of school to work full time for a technology company. Now, in 1999 making $15.00/hour was a lot of money. I was living a good life. Over the next several years, I worked at various companies in either a technology role or customer service position. As those years progressed, I attempted several times to go back to school. I would start a semester and attend for a few months and then leave again, feeling unfulfilled all the while. I was lost and had no clue what I wanted to do with my life. At some point I realized that I had a decision to make: figure out what I loved to do or keep going on the path I was on, doing work that left me constantly wanting more.

I've always had an entrepreneurial spirit, even though I didn't know one family member that had their own business. I attempted to become an entrepreneur on several occasions. The first time was when I was 14 years old and started doing hair. I was really awesome at it and had a good clientele that kept me in business at least part time all the way up until I was 22 years old. My second attempt at a business started when I was exposed to the janitorial world as a young adult. I started working under a family friend who mentored me, showing me how to bid for contracts with the state and win jobs. She was my first business mentor, and I learned a lot under her direction. I registered my business name and applied for an EIN (they weren't electronic back then), and then set about bidding for contracts of my own. I received one contract with my state, two housekeeping clients, and six apartment communities.

I attempted to run my janitorial business while I was working full-time, and needless to say, it was a disaster! I ended up getting fired from my job, because I was prioritizing my business even though I was making less money there. In addition to getting fired, a few months later I had to break my lease and move back home. Frustrated at what had happened, I decided at that time I no longer wanted to be an entrepreneur. Instead, I re-entered the rat-race, securing another job. This time, though, my job was flexible and allowed me to go to school. In 2010 I started school again part-time in a pre-med program at Eastern Michigan University. I was so excited to be in the program and was completing it with one of my good friends. However, it only took a dangling carrot to throw my focus off once again. I was presented me with an awesome opportunity with another company to make really good money and have awesome benefits. At that time, I felt like I was truly failing at life – so, instead of listening to my inner self and pursuing the education that I was truly passionate about, I decided to take another job with another company.

Anxiety and Depression

Nearly a decade later, I am still with this company. However, instead of just failing at life the way I was when I first started with this organization nine years ago, I have since found myself failing forward. Several years back, I started running an event decorating company part time. Things were going well until one day in August of 2017 when I was stuck in my tracks and hit by what I thought were the last days of my life. Here I was, driving down the highway laughing on the phone with a friend, when all of a sudden my heart started pounding, my mouth got super dry, and my breathing increased. Even though I am a licensed Emergency Medical Technician, I panicked and had no idea how to help myself in that moment. This was a scary feeling that I'd never experienced before, and the next exit was over a mile away. Still driving and in full on panic mode, I hit the red SOS button in my Chevy Malibu, because it was all I could think to do at the time. A lady came on to the speaker in the car, and calmly spoke with me as I struggled to explain what was happening to me and begging her to send help.

The last thing I can remember was waking up in the back of an ambulance. By the grace of God I was able to drive that additional mile and pull into a gas station before passing out. I was taken to a local hospital, where I was later released. For the next two and a half years I worked from a mental space of anxiety and depression. Even with medication, I still had ups and downs. Those ups and downs started to give me opportunities to learn some structure in my life. As you can probably tell from my story so far, I had really been living my life from an unplanned state. This experience and my diagnosis made it clear to me that I needed to gain control. I started to focus more on what my work life should be and how I should run my business.

Finding My Happy

As I worked through my anxiety and depression with my therapist I started to pay more attention to the decisions I was making and the next steps for my life. I was making six figures with my employer and running an event company that did decorating, handmade invitations, and balloon art. I knew I wanted to be an entrepreneur, but I also knew I wanted to provide stability for my children, so I sought ways to do that. Therapy helped me a lot with identifying the best strategies for this. I hadn't quite understood in 2017 why I had that anxiety attack, but I try not to question God's plan. What I did know was that if I wanted to continue to work my regular job and also build this business, I had to figure out how to do this without driving myself insane. I knew it would be a long road, but I was starting to find my happiness.

Over the next few years and to the present day, I continued to work to create a work-play-entrepreneurial balance in my life. Knowing that I wasn't quite ready to leave the working world entirely yet, I instead found a salary position that allowed me to be flexible enough with my children, but didn't have me working past 4:00 pm or on weekends. This was the perfect setup for me to change how I was operating in my business. Once I found my way at work, I started focus on how my business could be successful. Major decisions had to be made and it had to happen fast. In 2019, I decided to streamline my service offerings, removing decorating and custom invitations from my menu. Instead, we delved full force into balloon décor, but kept the name "Keita P. Designs."

2019 was our first year operating as only a balloon decor company and, like most entrepreneurs who start out, we had no clue what we were in store for. In 2020, my company had a slow start to the year and by the end of the first quarter we had to stop business completely due to COVID-19. I pondered for a month on how I could keep business going and level-up to ensure I had a fighting chance. I decided some additional education and training was in order, so I took my bonus check from work and invested into a mentoring program. During the six-week, intensive program I learned how to navigate the uncertain waters when your business has to pivot. I also did a rebrand to ensure that, if I decided later on that I wanted to sell my business, it had a name that resonated and could transition well to another owner. After all I am looking to be the Nike of balloons. So we changed our name from "Keita P. Designs" to Detroit Balloon Bar and upgraded our logo. By May 2020, I went from doing $1,000/month in sales to over $5,000. By the end of the year I had doubled my sales from 2019.

As we entered 2021, business wasn't slowing down, but we do have down seasons. To compensate for that, I decided it was time to add a retail component to my business. I started to forecast my sales, be more conscious about how money was flowing, work in my SEO (search engine optimization, and focus on who my ideal client was. To be sure that these things are not disrupted by others, I filed for a trademark to protect the investment I was making in my company. Sometimes all we need to be is a little organized to get a glimpse at what could be in store for us. Detroit Balloon Bar is now a six figure company and I did it all by working 5-9 and weekends. Now all I do is daydream about what my next level looks like. The only difference now is that I have the mental and physical tools to execute and make it happen!

Develop Your Plan

Kioshana LaCount Burrell
(Editor and Publisher)

Kioshana LaCount Burrell is a speaker, author, and career and lifestyle coach. She is the owner/operator of Thrifty Mama Media, LLC, an editing and publishing firm that specializes in providing space and guidance for amplifying the voices of everyday women. She has more than a decade of experience in career and life coaching, empowering clients to build careers that best serve the lifestyle that they desire. Her professional career spans the corporate, government, and higher-education sectors, but she is most happy when working individually with clients, enacting real, sustainable change in their everyday lives.

Connect with Kioshana:
Website: www.ThriftyMamaMedia.com
LinkedIn: https://www.linkedin.com/in/kioshanalacount/
Email: kioshana.lacount@gmail.com

Chapter Six: Building the Foundation for Your Entrepreneurial Success
Kioshana LaCount Burrell

As a budding entrepreneur, you may be feeling both exhilarated and overwhelmed. It is easy to get bogged down by all of the small, but somehow significant things that you "need" to be doing in order for your business to thrive. I hope that what you've learned from the other ladies in this book so far has given you some important insight into how you can identify and begin marketing to your ideal customers, establish boundaries and systems that allow for more "life" in your life/work balance, and at least begin thinking about the legacy that you intend to leave for those who come after you through your work.

I'd like to talk with you about some of the business basics people sometimes overlook when planning a launch, including some concrete steps that you need to take in order to get your business off on the right foot. Whether you are brand new to the entrepreneurship lifestyle, or have been growing in your business for a while but are maybe feeling a bit disorganized, these steps will help you get (and stay) on track.

Before diving in, however, allow me to first tell you a little bit about me. I am by trade, a career management professional. I began working as a career coach more than a decade ago, almost immediately after graduating from undergrad. Over the span of my career, I have held career counseling roles in the nonprofit, government, and higher education sectors. I have also had the great fortune to grow and evolve within my industry. My skill set has developed from primarily those of a career coach to now include project and team management, digital curriculum design, content creation, and more. Within the scope of career counseling, my approach has evolved as well. I now employ a philosophy of my own design when working with clients, and it is this philosophy that has allowed me to take on private career coaching clients even as I've been employed specifically as a career coach, and still avoid conflicts of interest with my primary job.

In order to successfully build a business (without losing your mind), you need to first do a few things to get your basics in alignment. Those basics are:

1. – Get your paperwork together
2. – Identify your "Remarkable Difference"
3. – Talk to your day job about your business

Before we even dive in to these three things, however, there is one other thing that you must do first. If the above mentions are Steps 1, 2, and 3, then you need to think of this other as Step Zero. I call this Step Zero because it is the single, most basic (yet profound) thing you can do to ensure your business' success. For Step Zero, you need to **adjust your mindset**.

Now, stay with me here – I know you've probably heard a lot about mindset in this and other similar books. However, I don't want you to underestimate the very real importance of this step. Your mindset must be set firm prior to undertaking any steps for your business, if you want a real chance at success. Whether you plan to continue working a 9-5 along with your business, or you endeavor to one day become a full time entrepreneur, it is critical that you approach your business planning from the mindset of someone who takes their business seriously. You must treat your business as an important and viable avenue for your success – otherwise, you will be hard pressed to actually realize success.

Personally, as an entrepreneur, I approach everything I do through that lens. I am a business owner 24 hours a day, and all of the work that I do is in service to (and considered through the lens of) that mindset. I even approach my 9-5 from the perspective of a business owner working with a client. As far as I'm concerned, my "day job" is work that I've been contracted to do through a "client" (my employer). This is helpful in maintaining some distance from my work, allowing me to enjoy my job but also helping me avoid becoming too attached to (and dependent on) that assignment. I allot time for my work duties as it relates to that "contract" and when my work day is done (and my obligations to my employer met for the day), I have no problem walking away from that work and focusing on any other clients or projects I'm currently contracted for in my business.

This mindset has been exceedingly beneficial to me as I have worked to grow my business into a viable and reliable source of income. It not only allows me to maintain healthy boundaries with my job, but it also ensures that I am always primed and ready for opportunities as they present themselves. In the words of the great Will Smith, "If you stay ready, you don't have to get ready."

So now that we've covered Step Zero, let's move on to the first of the three areas we will explore in this chapter: getting your paperwork together. As a business owner, it is imperative that you take the time to organize your business in the appropriate way, and then file the necessary paperwork to secure your business and yourself. Failure to do say may result in any number of emergencies later on down the road, including trademark issues, tax penalties, and more.

If you haven't already, take some time today and file for an EIN. An EIN (Employer Identification Number) is a tax designation that you file with the IRS to let them know that you have a business. Think of it as a social security number for your company. Many types of business grants and loans, as well as other activities you may undertake while working on your business, will require an EIN. Best of all, it's free to apply for, and you can have yours assigned and sent to you via email in a matter of minutes. Seriously – go file.

(https://www.irs.gov/businesses/small-businesses-self-employed/apply-for-an-employer-identification-number-ein-online)

You'll also want to take some time to decide on an incorporation status and secure it. As a small business, you're automatically designated as a sole proprietorship, unless you officially organize in a different capacity. Your options for designation are LLC, S-Corp (small corporation), and C-Corp (standard corporation). I won't go into the nuances of each type, but I will say that it is ill-advised to operate as a sole proprietorship. This is because, as a sole proprietor, you are personally responsible for any activities that your business undertakes. And if things ever go south with a client (or the government) and legal actions are taken, your personal assets are vulnerable (meaning, they can sue your "company" and take your actual money/things/etc.). If you're organized as an official business under one of the above designations, then the COMPANY is liable/vulnerable to legal actions, but you personally are protected. There are also several tax implications that come with organizing in different ways, so I suggest consulting with an attorney (or, at a minimum, get on RocketLawyer.com) and make a decision around that.

Finally, you'll want to research your local business licensing requirements. For some of you, it may be that you need a city or county business license (or both) in the area where your business is located. Even if you own a service-based business or work from your home instead of in a storefront, it is still advised that you obtain the appropriate licensure for your business (again, to avoid legal issues down the road).

Once you've taken care of the formal paperwork, you'll next want to concentrate on differentiating yourself. This is the step that I like to call "identifying your Remarkable Difference", in reference to an old marketing philosophy taught to me by Mr. Charlie Hardy, my first (and favorite) marketing professor at Alabama State University. Your Remarkable Difference is what makes you unique or special, and what sets you apart from your competition. You may have already begun this segment in the planning phase of your business organization, but you'll want to pay special attention to it as you begin to create (or recreate) marketing collateral for your business. Your Remarkable Difference should be something that is innate in your company, and something that is specific to you alone. It should be the basis of your overall branding, and for those who are pursuing business endeavors in the same industry as their day jobs, it is what sets you apart from the work that you do every day.

For example, I shared earlier that I am a career coach by trade, with more than a decade of career management experience. Although I have been gainfully employed as a career counselor (or similar) during this entire time, I also take on private clients. However, when working with private clients, I employ my own personal philosophy for career management, formed from my years of experience in the industry in general. I practice what I like to call "holistic career coaching" wherein I advise clients from the perspective of life/work balance. Notice that I say life/work balance instead of the typical "work/life" balance. That's because I don't subscribe to the idea that work should be the priority. Instead, I challenge clients to imagine their ideal life, and then together we develop strategies that support them in building a career that fits into that lifestyle (instead of the other way around).

I am also an unapologetic Job Snob ™ and I regularly work with clients in their job search strategizing with my SNOB method. SNOB is my own creation – it isn't something that an employer taught me. My holistic view of career management, as well as my use of SNOB (which is my own intellectual property) comprise my Remarkable Difference, and it is the reason that many people continue to work with me throughout the years. I challenge you to take a moment and think about what your Remarkable Difference is, and how you can leverage that difference to position yourself in a place of sustainability and winning in this season and beyond.

If you are an entrepreneur who is also still employed in a regular job, you'll at some point want to talk to your 9-5 about this new adventure you're embarking on. This step should come once you've done the work of formalizing the organization of your business and differentiating yourself strategically in your niche. While having this conversation isn't absolutely necessary, it is helpful in maintaining a strong relationship with your employer for as long as you remain employed at their business. Before diving in to the actual conversation, however, you'll want to prep (of course).

Begin by reviewing your employment contract, to ensure that you understand the nuances of the terms. Pay special attention to any clauses that discuss conflict of interest, outside employment, non-compete agreements, or intellectual property. Having a clear understanding of these components of your contract will allow you to fully understand what you can and cannot do in your business as it relates to your primary work, and will put you in a position of power when discussing your venture with your employer.

When you're ready to actually have the conversation with your employer, be as non-confrontational as possible. Be ready to communicate your Remarkable Difference (but only enough to show how you're different – don't give away all your sauce!), and most importantly, approach the conversation from a perspective of authority and clarity. Frame the conversation as, "This is something that I am committed to doing, so what do you need from me in order to be comfortable" instead of "How would you feel if I decided to do this?" Your business is just that – YOUR business. While you certainly don't want to be adversarial in your dealings with your boss, you should also realize that you don't need anyone's permission in order to go out on this adventure.

Just to recap: when you're looking to launch your own business (or even if you've been doing your own thing for a while) there are a few things you can do in order to give yourself the strongest foundation. First, you'll need to formally organize and get your paperwork in order. Then, you'll need to make sure that you have a clear understanding of, and ability to communicate, what it is that makes your business different (and therefore special). Finally, you'll need to have a candid conversation with your employer about your plans so that there is no room for misunderstanding about where your commitment lies.

Entrepreneurship is never an easy path, but it is infinitely worthwhile to craft something tangible and sustainable from what was once just an idea in your mind. Remember that you are not alone in this journey – we encourage you to build a tribe and connect with other like-minded women so that you can grow together with the support of your sisters. No matter what – never stop believing in your ability to do great things. Shine on, sis.

Veronica Marz

Mompreneur Extraordinaire. Full-time Badass. The original Haute Mess™.

Veronica is a mamabear to three amazing kiddos, an entrepreneur, and the creator of the Bad Bxtch Club Podcast. She is also an American author, inspirational storyteller, and personal development expert.

Aspiring beauty maven who loves all things coffee, makeup, books, yoga, and fitness. Free spirit, raising three babies, going crazy. Her house is like all the most eclectic Marvel characters you can think of under one roof. Always fun.

Connect with Veronica:

Website: https://msha.ke/veronicamarz/
Twitter: https://twitter.com/veronicamarzxx
Instagram: https://www.instagram.com/veronicamarzxx/
TikTok: https://www.tiktok.com/@veronicamarzxx

Chapter Seven:
The Art of Failing
Veronica Marz

If you had told me ten years ago that in 2021 I would be a divorced single mother, happily pursuing her life's passions as a successful entrepreneur, while healing traumas and bending reality to her every whim, I would have undoubtedly called you a liar. This isn't a typical "Rags to Riches" story, not yet anyway. I didn't have a father that could give me a small loan of a million dollars. No silver spoons, or nepotism over here. As much as I'd like to think my success is in most part due to luck-- I know that it isn't. My success is by design. That design has one major component that turns me into a well-oiled machine when I am in 'creation mode'. That component is failure.

In the personal development world, we hear a lot about 'failing forward', but sometimes failing forward will have you tripping on your own feet, unable to catch your breath, burnt out and overwhelmed... Whew, child... the GHETTO! (said in my best Nene Leaks voice). In the year of our Lord, 2021, we are no longer failing forward to stumble without being able to catch our breath. Instead, let's coin a new term: Failing upward. In this chapter, I'm going to take you on a short journey with me to discuss all of my insecurities and failures, and how I took those failures to ascend to the high heavens despite the odds.

Sidenote: You will get cuts and bruises while breaking glass ceilings, trust me.

In 2019, I made the leap from full time employee to full time entrepreneur. Having had the courage to finally go down the road less taken did NOT automatically mean success and money. I had to fight for every inch of success I got. To this day, I still fight hard for the success I have. Every follower, comment, connection...all of it. By fight, I mean work. I previously held an administrative title, doing disaster relief outreach work for a very well known American Non-Profit company. While a large portion of this work was challenging, yet rewarding, it was not rewarding in my life in ways that enriched my life. This position took so much out of me mentally and emotionally. I was depleted, completely defeated (I love making accidental rhymes), and ready for more-- But for MONTHS I was too fucking afraid to really go after what I wanted. I'll tell you what broke me: a bad breakup, my boss forgetting my birthday, and finally being tired... Of being sick and tired. In the grand scheme of things, those items are very nominal, but when the Divine is calling you for a greater purpose, you start to see things in a different light.

The fear of failing *again* is what stopped me from going after all those things I really wanted. I had to learn how to harness the power of my fear, and let that mold me into the woman I have become now. I am constantly learning and growing. I am always looking deeply at those things that I was not good at in the past, and reverse engineering them so that I can be better in the future. I have three failed businesses under my belt. I've tried time and time again to really make a serious break into the acting industry, and for years I had no clue how to build a following or find my target market. It would take years of learning graphic design on my own, late nights studying marketing, and a lot of reaching out to people who did not care to help me for me to realize that the greatest tool I have is myself.

   If you want to learn how to fail upward, you have to learn how to look at yourself in the mirror and acknowledge all of your headaches and hang-ups and face those things head on. Conquering your own fears and insecurities is something no one will ever be able to take from you. It will be one of the single greatest things that will give you power and propel you into a new life --- the life you've always wanted and dreamed of. That's where you start, with yourself. Analyze the deeper meaning behind why certain things don't work out for you, especially if it's always the same certain thing. Learn to be comfortable sitting with yourself, in stillness. I don't mean to sound cliché', but yes, you need to meditate and do some yoga… cause it works. Once you can start to look at your failures and insecurities without feeling cringe or embarrassment, that's when you are well on your way to changing your own reality. Like most other skills we acquire, failing upward will take time to learn. The goal isn't perfection, the goal is continuously mastering ourselves. You don't have to be the best to be successful. You only need to be 1% better than everyone else. This is tried and true.

My very first business stepping outside of a 9 to 5 was an apparel brand I created in 2017 geared toward female entrepreneurs. The designs were great, and I knew that because several people who made regular purchases of these designs gave me that feedback. But my execution was horrible and disorganized. I did not promote enough. I was inconsistent with social media posts. I was terrible at delegation and so afraid that others were going to steal my brand that I rarely hired help unless it was something I absolutely couldn't do on my own. I was happy to have made a few dollars, but it was a bomb. A big one.

I was able to name the things I failed at (delegation, organization, social media, and marketing) because I spent a lot of time after the dissolution of that business thinking about what I could do better next time, no matter what business I created. After realizing what I was doing wrong, I took action. I began working on a new business venture, and tried to incorporate new skills I had learned into that business. It was also a failure (HA!) but the point I am trying to make is that you have to get comfortable with the idea of failing, and not let that hinder or deter you from the next thing that may ultimately work out. With this second business, I failed at identifying what my target market should have been (again, disorganized af) and because of that many of the online marketing campaigns and ads failed. I spent hundreds marketing to no one, because Facebook damn sure wasn't showing my ads... but I didn't tell Facebook who I needed to see those ads. (I also had a notebook where I kept a lot of business notes about this. I watched Shark Tank a lot, but that should NOT be a substitution for doing your own research!! Don't be lazy).

There were many hiatuses between ventures. Many moments to stop and reflect. I realized I was tripping on my own feet and that what I needed to do is learn how to walk to success instead of always trying to run to it. I started working on myself, doing the inner work. Finding systems that worked better for my artistic and whimsical mind. Systems that could help me stay more organized within my business, cause this free spirit inside me don't give a s*** about being organized. I had to teach myself some new things, and it was hard in the beginning. But 30 days makes a habit, right? That and keeping my 'Why?' in the forefront of my mind. I am the first college graduate in my family. The first successful entrepreneur. I am determined to be the first millionaire in my family. I am still trying to figure out what drives this train inside of me to always want to break the barriers. But I stopped questioning and became laser focused on improvements. When I did, I began to see results. Taking action, and applying new knowledge after dissecting perceived failure is what brought me closer to success.

On that note…

The road to success is not linear. It's more like a rip current in the ocean. More predictable than not, but if you try to guess what it's next move is, you'll most likely be wrong. Success is a calculation. A math equation. X = Failure. Find X and you find your success. Failure isn't the bad guy. Failure is the path that can show us the way to success. It's our light in the dark. Remember that the next time you are trying to figure out your next move. You are playing a game of chess against yourself. (Chess sucks, IMHO) Failure is your cheerleader. You have to know every inch of yourself, even the bad parts, if you want to win. You are your own competition. These things you will have to know and do if you intend to survive outside of a standard 9 to 5. I hope that you slay every goal you make, and fail upward with grace along the way.

Marci Bryant, MBA

Marci Bryant, MBA is a Customer Experience Strategist from Detroit, MI. As the founder of SYNC Digital Agency, she helps STEM companies design digital systems that align customer facing teams through omnichannel communications and technology.

Her corporate career includes 25 years of marketing, sales and service in automotive, manufacturing, healthcare, fitness, retail, media, and telecommunications industries. She currently works as a technical copywriter in the automotive industry.

Marci is also a contributing writer for Career Mastered magazine, founder of Black Digital Designers, and mother of one amazing toddler.

Connect with Marci:

LinkedIn: https://www.linkedin.com/in/marcibryantmba/
Facebook: https://www.facebook.com/MarciBryantMBA/
Instagram: https://www.instagram.com/marcibryantmba/
Website: https://www.marcibryantmba.com

Chapter Eight: The Season of Success
Marci Bryant, MBA

Have you ever felt the gravity of your elevation to success? It reminds me of the slow climb up a roller coaster. I feel the tightness of the harness across my chest. I hear the tick-tick-tick of the roller coaster gears moving beneath me. I feel the wind in my hair as I move higher into the sky. I feel the sun in my eyes, even with closed lids, as the cart inches upward ever so slowly. I feel the nervousness as the coaster stops suddenly at the top of the hill - giving me one final chance to mentally prepare for the dips and curves - before it jerks ahead at full speed into exhilarating, crazy fun!

In the latest season of my life, I have been tick-tick-ticking up that roller coaster. Today, I am finally at the top of the hill. After sacrifice, survival, and struggle - I've finally arrived at the season of success, on my own terms. To anyone on the outside looking in, it might seem like a windfall of good luck has just been bestowed upon me suddenly. The truth is, this season has arrived because I have worked tirelessly to expand my talents over the past 25 years, intentionally positioning myself for success in both my career and business.

For a long time, I felt torn between growing my business and growing my career. Figuring out how to synchronize the skills and lessons from each of those worlds in order to excel in both spaces has been the key to my professional growth. There were many days that I dreamt of working from home in a fulfilling role while being a stay-at-home mom, evolving entrepreneur, and professional speaker. I have found a way to do all of these things - and it brings me even more joy than I thought possible.

In my professional career, I'm returning to Corporate America as a Technical Copywriter for a software startup in the automotive industry. In my business, I'm building digital systems that transform the customer experience for STEM companies by synchronizing their marketing, sales, and service processes. I'm building my brand authority as a professional speaker by sharing my expertise in magazines, blogs, podcast interviews, anthologies, and industry workshops. I'm now exactly where I want to be in my life and career – let's talk for a bit about how I got here, and some things that I learned along the way.

Sacrifice

I remember being asked what I wanted to be when I grew up. I always knew that I wanted to write commercials. My creative interests came from my mother's work at our local TV station. I spent many days after school learning about production, journalism, and advertising.

I made my career aspirations known with the producers and my mother helped me get cast in a commercial for one of their clients in third grade. Shortly after the commercial was released, I was invited to participate in a filmed Christmas special with a larger speaking role. Our segment was recorded in a historic mansion with Isiah Thomas, a member of the Detroit Pistons. Those two experiences solidified my career goals in marketing and media at an early age. Shortly after that, I started reading poetry books and studying writers, winning awards for my own poetry by seventh grade.

I graduated from college with big dreams and even bigger ideas about what it took to get to my dream job of writing commercials. I was under the mistaken impression that my experiences would allow me to break right into the advertising industry as a copywriter. I had those early TV experiences, along with 3 internships completed by the time I completed my Bachelor's degree in Advertising. However, the industry shifted and agencies were looking for designers who could write. But I wasn't a designer, I was a writer. And advertising graduates with less than two years of agency experience ended up in sales or customer service, which I never wanted to do.

Sales felt pushy and stressful. Customer service felt micro-managed and suffocating. In spite of my disdain for the roles, I achieved great success in those customer-facing positions before I burnt out. In my last customer service role, I was so stressed that I was on disability for nearly nine months. I was weak and fatigued, on bed rest for weeks at a time, and lost massive weight due to anxiety impacting my digestive system.

My bills were piling up and I was on the verge of homelessness. I did know that I would rather lose it all than work one more day in the capacity that I had been for my entire career. By then I had my MBA in Marketing and I was desperate to break free from these roles. I'd been with three companies and none had seen my potential to promote me from the customer-facing position into an advertising or marketing role.

My only marketing success over the years had come from taking on independent contractor roles to manage and train promotional teams for fitness and retail brands. I knew I needed to reposition myself, so I took some time to review my credentials, declare STEM as my niche, and invested in a full resume revision.

Armed with my new resume, I set out on a new job search, but found myself still facing roadblocks because I was lacking design experience. Here was the same minimum qualification still showing up after all these years, but I finally found out how much it was costing me to not have these necessary industry skills. I lost out on an $80k job opportunity when the hiring manager realized I didn't have this experience. I was so close to changing my life, but I wasn't prepared for the opportunity so I lost it. After that setback, I had to figure out a new plan so that I could find the success that I so badly desired. I had all these skills, but there was a glaring hole in my proficiency that I had knowingly allowed myself to have. After spending some time, I realized that this deficit was rooted in one thing: fear of failure.

I recalled as a child being selected for a gifted and talented art program. Although I was successful in creating beautiful art during that experience, I never fully accepted the idea that I was actually *good* at art (although I wanted to be). Reflecting further, I realized that all throughout my education and career I'd consciously avoided every opportunity to learn design because it felt like art, and I believed that I wasn't an artist. And by that time, I didn't even necessarily want to be. I just wanted to be a writer that worked with designers to create ads. Instead of pursuing this skillset, I'd decided to pursue an MBA, thinking that attaining more business acumen would get me to my big break. What I actually needed to do was face my fear of failure as an artist and become a digital designer.

Right then and there I decided that I would stop being afraid of my own talent – instead, I would hone in on that artistry and leverage it to become a successful digital designer. I vowed to face my fear of failure head-on to focus solely on learning the skills required to become a designer. Within 30 days I was enrolled in college again, this time as an online digital design student at The Art Institute of Pittsburgh.

I must admit, I was terrible at first and I didn't understand much. At that time, I was still facing some debilitating health problems, and my illness and low energy made it even more difficult to focus. I spent many days slumped over my computer crying and banging on the keyboard because I was having difficulty getting the design results I needed. But, after every tantrum, I gathered myself and got back to work. I pushed myself, even against physical limitations, because I knew what was possible for me on the other side of this challenge.

Within 2 months of my enrollment at the Art Institute, I learned enough basic design skills to land my first role as a corporate marketing director with a privately owned automotive company. Those small contracts with big titles coupled with my new design skills helped me write my own ticket. I was able to choose my own salary, set my relocation benefit amount, get approval for telecommuting 20% of the month, receive immediate medical benefits, and many other work-related perks. They gave me everything I needed to relocate and set up in a new state within three weeks!

The position allowed me to single-handedly run all marketing, advertising, and sales training efforts for this multi-million dollar company. My work was suddenly in regional and national publications. I was writing, designing, and producing print ads, radio ads, and TV commercials. I was managing graphic designers, videographers, producers, journalists, account managers, vendors, sponsors, talent, and trade show logistics.

I was also tasked with being the face of my department, including traveling to trade shows and industry expos on behalf of the company. Oftentimes I was the youngest professional in the room, the only person of color, and one of very few women in the space. I wore that triple minority like a badge of honor. A girl from Detroit with a customer service and sales background moved to Indiana to run marketing for a rural-based, automotive industry leader. Many people were perturbed, and even uncomfortable, at how I got the job with no automotive experience. My reply was always, "I might be new to automotive, but I know marketing - and marketing is what got me here."

I quickly learned that being in this industry, in this part of the country meant that I needed to develop a thick skin. I encountered countless racist and sexist incidents during my time with the company, and even found myself being harassed by other expo or hotel patrons at times. In spite of these uncomfortable events, I pressed on with my work because I knew what this job would do for my resume and career.

Survival

Unfortunately, my mother became terminally ill less than a year into my new job in a new state. I was alone in my apartment when I found out that, after several years in remission, her cancer had returned. Crying myself to sleep with no support system around me, I realized how lonely it can sometimes be to follow your dreams. I still had to keep working as though nothing had changed - even though most of my weekends were spent traveling 11 hours round trip to visit her back home and care for her, while still trying to maintain my studies and household in just 4 days a week. After months of road running and state-to-state caregiving, I had to put my career on hold to focus on my family. I moved back home to care for my mother just over a year after relocating for the job, while finishing design school. Although it was challenging to stay focused on both school and my caregiving responsibilities, it brought both of us great joy that she was still here to see me accomplish that goal.

She passed one month after I graduated with a 3.98 - my highest GPA ever - and her obituary was the first thing I created as an officially certified digital designer. I used my new skill set to tell her story in exactly the way my brother and I saw fit, but quickly became overwhelmed with depression in the weeks after the funeral reflecting on all that I had lost. Gone was my good job, my beautiful apartment, my car - which got repossessed as I was enrolling my mother in hospice - my mother, and then my mother's apartment, and then my mother's car. In order to survive the darkness, I had to shift my focus to gratefulness. I worked hard to figure out what I gained during that harrowing experience, so that I could pick up the remaining pieces of my life and move forward.

As I reflected, I realized I had gained a lot. I gained confirmation from the industry about my marketing and sales training skills. I gained a strong design portfolio from my class assignments and recent work. I gained a legacy of my passion for media from my mother. I gained a plethora of new skills from earning two degrees and a new digital design certification. I gained a new ability to manage clients and agency partners. I gained a fresh start with an opportunity to set and conquer new goals. I decided that I wanted to start my own business. It was the best way for me to find something positive to focus on and create income during a time that I was working with limited resources. It was also a tribute to my mother for believing in my dreams and helping me to achieve my career goals. Losing my mother made me think a lot about my legacy, and I was more inspired than ever to have my work become part of my legacy through my entrepreneurial journey.

I created a brand name, logo, website, business cards, flyers, vertical and vinyl banners, and secured affiliate partnerships with various marketing software companies. I learned so much during that creation process that I ended up using those skills to build the service offerings for my marketing business.

In the following months, I started to gain business clients from networking in small business circles, and I easily became disinterested in my original business model. I spent lots of time talking to people and they would tell me all these grand dreams of magnificent marketing campaigns, and most times they either wanted to barter or had less than $200 to spend. While I was grateful for anyone who trusted me with their business as a marketing professional, I still couldn't help feeling like I was meant to do more lucrative business deals than what I was actually doing at that time. I realized that even though I was a small business and a new entrepreneur, that wasn't actually who I wanted to work with.

I started feeling bitterness towards my business because everything I designed seemed to take so long and customers were extremely difficult to satisfy. When I calculated all the hours I spent on design and revisions versus my rates I realized that I was making less than minimum wage. I was frustrated and got burnt out again - this time from my own creation. I knew that I wasn't satisfied with my results or the type of customer that I was creating, but even as a marketer I couldn't figure out how to change what was happening. I was ready to attract people who had big dreams for their business and actually had the resources to implement their marketing goals.

I decided that in order to really evolve in my business, I needed to have some more success in Corporate America. So, after 2 years away from "work", I decided to get another job.

Struggle

I interviewed and was offered a role as Marketing Communications Coordinator with a new company. I was only able to secure 75% of my previous salary, which was understandably disappointing, but I needed the work to survive and the experience to grow, so I accepted the role. I had been dreaming about working with marketing automation software and managing a large digital customer experience project, and was now positioned to do just that. I was promised managerial opportunities and a raise to my previous salary as the department grew if I accomplished the deliverables set forth in the very large goal. I was given six months and $100,000 to accomplish the goal. I was able to negotiate everything they needed and some bonus print-marketing materials for in-person sales and trade shows. The project stayed within budget and deadline and brought in $240,000 within four months.

Despite that, I was not offered a review, promotion, bonus, or rate increase. Although the Vice President of Sales was satisfied, it seemed that he was not on the same page as the CEO. A holdover from a pre-acquisition version of the company, she was used to the "old way" of doing things and was hesitant to believe in marketing automation to differentiate and scale the business in a way that in-person sales alone could not. Instead of delivering on the verbal promises I'd been made in return for my success, she decided to remove me from my previous team and hired a customer service leader with no marketing experience to manage me.

To add insult to injury, I was relocated to this new customer service leader's office and instructed to train him. He hardly paid attention as I thoroughly trained him on the software and processes that I had spent the last year building and perfecting. During our first campaign launch under his leadership, he overlooked a few misspelled words while editing one of our marketing materials (now his responsibility after ridding me of my official editor). Because I was the originator of the material, however, I was written up for the mistake – even though it was not my responsibility to approve articles for production. I knew then that it was time to move on.

Two weeks later, around lunchtime, I submitted my immediate resignation to our HR department. I'd already secured a new position (along with an $18k salary increase) and didn't need to spend any more of my time or talent on this company that had treated me so poorly. My new role was a Communications Specialist focused on Systems Engineering in product development for a manufacturing company. It was a contract position where I worked onsite for the client and was integrated into the space like an employee.

While working on the concept of systems engineering I learned about cross-functional collaboration through teams, frameworks, and software. It was during my work to communicate this to the product development engineers globally that I was able to see exactly what was wrong with my business. I had the tools to be successful, but my framework was underdeveloped and it was affecting my confidence which caused me to attract low-paying customers. I realized that I was afraid to operate in my expertise as a business owner, even though I operated in my expertise daily as an employee or contractor. I left that role a year later, inspired to begin anew with my business.

Success

I spent another two years away from work starting a family and building my business. I spent plenty of time applying the lessons I learned about systems engineering to build my own marketing systems and framework. I hired a business coach to help me with positioning and processes. I had studied the business coach's content and free digital products for nearly three years before I hired her. When I made the decision to hire her, I was completely unemployed and had very little activity in my business. My biggest regret was that I hadn't made this decision sooner, but I had to come to my own enlightenment in my own divine timing.

I believed that if I could just have enough for one payment to access the information, that I would not be worried about the other 11 payments. I enrolled knowing that I only had enough for one payment, and within that first month I landed a new contract with the same manufacturer in a different department with a $20k raise over the previous role. In order to land that role, I relied heavily on the positioning work I had done with my business coach in the first two weeks, along with a versatile portfolio that I amassed throughout my professional career and entrepreneurial endeavors. Within two months, I also landed my first 5-figure client.

COVID-19 caused me to lose 20% of my salary for more than a year due to furlough. During that time, I started to look for new opportunities. I didn't even want my old role back at full-time anymore. I was ready to take on new challenges so when I finally saw my dream job as a copywriter for an automotive software owned by the same manufacturer, I applied. I received an interview and after a few weeks, I received an offer via email that almost made me fall off the couch when I read it! They willingly offered me so much more than I asked for and gave me so much more than I even knew to ask for. I went from unemployed to six figures in under two years, and I earn approximately double the median salary for my title because of my diverse business and marketing experience, along with my STEM expertise. I was brought in at the highest level of the individual contributor roles, so any promotion with this company automatically puts me in a leadership position.

During the time that I was interviewing, I started moving as if the job was already mine. I started refining my frameworks for digital products, group coaching, corporate training, and VIP Days. I hired a team of four apprentices to assist me with completing my client workload and supporting my restructuring efforts. I had a rebranding photoshoot and landing page redesign for my personal brand. I created and curated months-worth of social media content and developed a Facebook group dedicated to helping Black Digital Designers go from struggling artists to high-paid creative professionals.

This season of success has arrived because I worked tirelessly for decades to perfect my craft, both in my business and in my career. This time I was prepared for great opportunities, and I was rewarded with achieving my lifelong goal of becoming a technical copywriter in Corporate America.

Porché Maloney

Porché Maloney is a dynamic and inspiring brand strategist and human resources expert. Proudly hailing from the great city of Pittsburg, PA, Porché is a resourceful young professional with a history of contributing top-tier diverse talent to company and client pipelines. Porché describes herself as a servant leader at heart, as evidenced by both her career and entrepreneurial accomplishments. She founded her business, Design Haven Studio, in the midst of the COVID-19 pandemic. Her mission has been to leverage her innate understanding of talent attraction to support small businesses grow through the challenges and changes presented by the pandemic with thoughtful and innovative brand strategy and web design solutions. Porché is the quintessential millennial entrepreneur, proving daily that you're never too young to make an indelible impact on the world around you

At Design Haven Studio, we are always accepting new clients and would love to create brand building solutions for you - visit us at www.designhavenstudio.com. Special thanks to the Design Haven Studio client family, we appreciate your business!

Connect with Porché:

Website: www.designhavenstudio.com
Instagram: https://www.instagram.com/design_haven_studio/
Facebook: https://www.facebook.com/designhavenstudio
LinkedIn: https://www.linkedin.com/in/porchemaloney/

Chapter Nine: Becoming... Ms. Corporate-preneur
Porché Maloney

Picture this...

You are a young, doe-eyed, fresh faced, 20-something Black woman from the inner city of Pittsburgh. You learned early on that nothing is given, nor promised. Through a combination of prayer and pulling yourself up by your bootstraps, you've been able to fulfill your aspirations to "make it out" and achieve the big dreams you have so far. You have always been willing to put in the WORK to make things happen. This is how you got into some of the best colleges in the country, earned scholarships, were selected for pristine internships and other leadership opportunities while graduating with multiple degrees. Sounds like life worked out well and all is pretty smooth sailing right? This is where my career began, and I must admit that, for a while, things were better than I could have imagined. I was on top of the world, making the kind of boss moves I always knew that I would. Little did I know, though, that the shake-up was imminent.

Before we reach the climax however, let's get back to the climb...

Now that you're in the "real world" with your business degrees, everything seems to be falling into place. The introduction to Corporate America has so far been great. You've been hired by one of the biggest global companies (a name recognizable in everyone's household) and you're building up your network on a daily basis. Through it all you are also experiencing the perks of having supportive mentors and coaches that look like you, looking out for you. Even the VP of Human Resources knows your name (for all the right reasons).

This was the genesis of my career, my introduction to the professional world. In a very short period of time, I was able to create connections and quickly ascend the ranks in my career, surpassing even my own expectations. I recall feeling as though everything I wanted was just within my reach. Then one day, I watched everything fall apart around me.

All at once, everything about my work world changed irrevocably. I rapidly went from having a "work-hard and build connections = career growth guaranteed" mentality to witnessing and experiencing first-hand some of Corporate America's darkest horror stories. Suddenly, going into the office each day felt more like going into the Hunger Games – and we never had any indication about who would be selected as a sacrificial tribute.

Imagine trying to function at work while experiencing any of following around you day-to-day:

1. Job uncertainty brought about because of company mergers & acquisitions

2. Seeing fully-staffed office's turn into ghost towns due to a 30,000+ employee layoff, job eliminations and entire business unit closures

3. Watching 20+ year company veterans forced into early retirement and essential senior leaders leaving the corporation left and right

4. Witnessing one of America's core corporations, crash and fall off the stock market all in a matter of two years

It goes without saying this is a lot to take in all at once. Going from the easy breezy corporate life to never knowing if you're next on the chopping block can take a toll on your mental and emotional health. What's even more upsetting is that any of these instances can become sad realities for anyone that is classified as an employee. Time and time again, I've seen qualified, competent and accomplished people (especially those of Color) play the corporate game by the book and still end up on the losing end. Playing the game alone leaves no room to create a legacy or build generational wealth because the business's bottom line trumps everything. Luckily, I learned this lesson early on in my career, and as a result, I decided I wanted more.

FUEL for Your WHY...

You may have heard this term discussed elsewhere, and I hope that my story emphasizes for you the criticality of building something beyond a regular, every day job.

Corporate-preneur (/ˈkôrp(ə)rət -prəˈnər /): "one who maintains a full-time 9-5 career, while simultaneously growing a business of their own."

The truth is, as a working individual, you never truly experience "job security". One day everything could be going fine professionally and the next you're in the middle of a global pandemic; witnessing millions of people file for unemployment and close their places of business. My remedy is to engage in multiple **REVENUE GENERATING** activities, ensuring that I never need to depend on one stream of income for my livelihood. The 9-5 and 5-9 life is the way for me.

Trust that it will be a process. Corporate-preneurs experience a plethora of peaks and valleys, wins and losses but in the end, it is well worth the ride.

Finding Your Niche...

As a true servant leader, I've always had a passion for sowing back into others. My 9-5 allows me to do exactly that on a grander scale. Currently, I help underserved minorities develop dynamic personal brands, gain access to meaningful career opportunities and close the achievement gap across the workplace.

Assisting others with personal & professional brand development has always been a sweet spot for me. My entrepreneurial endeavors also involve sowing these seeds into emerging and established business owners. Hence the birth of Design Haven Studio; we are the one-stop shop for brand building solutions.

Your business activities don't always have to be in the field of what you formally studied or were trained to do. I find owning my own business to be a refreshing release that allows my creativity to thrive in the form of website/logo design, creating marketing materials, social media content creation and more. I did not pigeon-hole myself into thinking I had to stay in my respective lane; I put forth the time and energy to identify a path that would be both challenging and fulfilling, ultimately choosing to pursue a website design certificate. Each project I undertake brings about unique nuances that teach and inspire me, pushing me to **"go farther, go further, go harder. Is that not why we came? And if not, then why bother?"** - Jay-Z

Build, Grow and Scale Your Niche...

Not sure where to get started when it comes to identifying your path? Don't worry, I can help. Special thanks to my business coaches and mentors for being a part of the journey that included the following steps:

1. **Self-Reflection**

Get to know yourself. Conduct a SWOT (Strengths, Weaknesses, Opportunities and Threats) Analysis. Make a list of your likes and dislikes as it pertains to life and professional matters. Take inventory on what you do well and your areas of improvement. Think about what skills you may have developed but haven't tapped into. For example, I jotted down a few of my technical skills and was reminded that I learned how to build websites in college. I dusted off those skills years later and created Design Haven Studio, a rather lucrative business endeavor.

> Quotable Equivalent: "Work That. Be yourself, Work What You Got"- Mary J. Blige

2. **Mentor and Coach Engagement**

Throughout your life and career you may be blessed to have a person or people that are truly dedicated to seeing you succeed. These people will see your growth, be your sounding board, serve as a beacon of inspiration and help you navigate through the highs and lows. Tap into your mentor and coach resources as they can provide advice and insight on identifying what you do best, and what you can build on successfully.

Quotable Equivalent - "Your Network is Your Net Worth" - Porter Gale

3. **Aptitude Test & Assessments**

I am a huge advocate for performance and personality assessments. Whether it is DISC, Welcome to the Jungle, Myers-Briggs or any other assessment, the results shed amazing insight on the following:

- How you can best interact with others
- Environments that would allow you to excel
- Predictive behaviors and personality traits

Heightened self-awareness will enable you to speak your truth and understand the value you bring to the table.

Quotable Equivalent: "Know Yourself, Know Your Worth" - Drake

4. **Personal Development Investments**

Invest in yourself like you would and should in your business. For example, you can invest in yourself by attending development and leadership conferences or workshops and earning specialty certifications.

Applying the knowledge and skills acquired during these activities are bound to earn a sizable return-on-investment.

Quotable Equivalent -"Believe in and Bet on Yourself to Win" - Nipsey Hustle

Hopefully sharing this will shed light on how you too can step out on faith and find your passion. Solely being a worker bee is not the end-all be-all. I encourage you to tap into your genius zone, find the path that works for you, and create diversity in your work and life.

Special Thanks…

This short snippet of my story is dedicated to my mother - the person always telling me to write a book for all the times I'd call and say, "Hey mom – you're never gonna believe this!"

I'm thankful for this platform and hope it inspires the next aspiring entrepreneur to realize:

"Don't just fight for or be satisfied with a seat at the table, strive to build your own simultaneously."

Cassie Catrice

Cassie Catrice is a Global Talent Development Consultant at Cassie Catrice Consulting where she helps companies create a supportive ecosystem to maintain diverse talent. Cassie has extensive experience creating interdisciplinary projects that have lasting impact. She is a graduate of the University of Illinois at Urbana Champaign with a Masters in Human Resources and Industrial Relations, a Certificate in Business Administration, and a Bachelor's in Sociology with a concentration in Organizational Communication and Leadership.

Connect with Cassie:

Website: www.CassieCatriceConsulting.com
Employment: cassiecatrice.jobs@gmail.com
Bookings: CassieCatrice@cassiecatriceconsulting.com
Instagram: https://www.instagram.com/cassie_catrice/
Facebook: https://www.facebook.com/CassieCatriceConsulting
LinkedIn: https://www.linkedin.com/in/cassiecatrice/

Chapter Ten:
Level Up Your Leadership - Become a Career Competent and Confident Leader
Cassie Catrice

If you picked up this book and are reading this chapter, you probably did so because you are an ambitious high-achieving woman who wants it all including a vibrant career, a joy filled life, and a path where having a purpose beyond your current job feels possible. You may even already have it all by society's standards. Yet, you still find yourself feeling misaligned, unfulfilled, wanting more in life, feeling overworked, overwhelmed, or over stressed at times. You may be in a space where life feels like a marathon where you are checking off all of the external boxes and accolades but not fully enjoying the run. You are here because you are wanting to feel more confident while achieving your ambitious goals with balance and ease. You want show up more confidently at whatever stage you are in the process regardless of how imperfect or messy life, career, the business gets. You want to feel like someone else gets you because you may be the only person in your circle who is operating with the intention of moving beyond your 9-5. I am here to say to you, "I get you. I feel you. I see you. I am you."

The good news is that the very fact that you're reading this book means you believe in yourself and I believe in you too. You believe in more and are eager to find an alternative way to how you are currently approaching these things today. You are searching for ideas, tools, a strategy, and systems that work; you may even be longing for a community that would support you in the growth process. Hopefully, by the end of this chapter, I will be able to provide you with a deeper understanding and awareness around decisions and actions that you can begin implementing today to move you closer towards the life you want which includes a robust purposeful business and a joy-filled life, as well as a path to attain these things and more with confidence, balance, and ease.

To that end, I invite you to **Level Up Your Leadership and Become a Career Competent & Confident Leader** with me. On this self-improvement ("Level Up") journey, you do not need to feel as though you have to subscribe to the belief that you're alone or that you need to be a superwoman. On this journey of elevating and transforming yourself professionally and personally, it is completely okay (in fact, it is welcomed) to ask for help. It is also okay to not have all the answers or feel as though you need to be a superwoman. Now that we have addressed that, let your Level Up begin!

As you level up, you become a better version of yourself. You show up differently in your career, business, leadership and life. This impacts your ability to competently and confidently pursue your goals. You become what I refer to as a **Career Competent & Confident Leader,** which I define as an expert in a specialized domain who is equipped to deliver the work (competent). This expert is aware of their strengths and blindspots that could impact their individual progress or that of their team and takes actions to maximize opportunities and reduce risk. A key differentiator between a Career Competent Leader and other leaders is that in conjunction with possessing the expertise, a Career Competent & Confident Leader also exudes the confidence to lead themselves and empower their team to strategically carry out the vision in a progressive, sustainable, and scalable way.

Becoming a Career Competent & Confident Leader requires a new strategy and tools that will help you and your team grow, transform, and accomplish more intentional actions with more alignment and ease. Sure there will be an adjustment period initially that will require at the minimum a time investment and likely also a financial investment. However, it will be well worth the investment to reach your highest potential in your career, business, and life. Ready? Let's get started.

Before I share with you more about my journey, I first would like to tell you about how Cassie Catrice Consulting came to life. I stood up my boutique consulting agency from a space and desire to give back. I have always had a passion for helping people reach their goals and potential in life as early as grammar school when I ran for and became class and student body president. This trend continued through high school and college when I started a student organization and facilitated workshops for peers on self-improvement. I have always enjoyed learning and growing and had an affinity for problem solving, being a change-agent, and sharing my learnings and resources with those who were also invested in themselves and eager to learn and grow. Today, I incorporate elements of fashion, professional branding, and health in my Talent Strategy and Career Coaching programs which you can learn more about on my website at www.cassiecatriceconsulting.com

Managing Generational Bias in the Workforce
(*Or, Thriving as a Millennial Gal in a Multi-Generational Corporate World*)

Having stepped into leadership earlier in life, at many points throughout my life and my career, I was faced with a decision around how I would balance my time, responsibilities, priorities, myself, my emotions, and lead and be in relationship with others. It was a responsibility that I did not always do perfectly. I made and learned from my mistakes. The biggest misconception about that I have had to work to overcome has been around what I can or cannot do because of my perceived age and the generation to which I belong.

More times than I can count, I have been met with "What do you know?", "Aren't you a little young to be giving advice?," "I'm going to listen to someone with more experience".... Or my favorite (not so) favorite - when they disregard what you say completely and listen to another individual who says the same thing – especially when those individuals fall outside of a younger generation.

I have found myself speaking up about ageist bias in professional situations, as well as having to account for and make adjustments for the conscious and unconscious biases of others. While it is not always ideal, this has challenged me to become a better advocate for myself, better articulate my strengths and experiences, and creatively compose a variety of ways to storytelling and illustrate my portfolio to a diverse audience.

Though I do not change everyone's mind (nor do I set out to), being aware of the role that age bias plays in the workplace can better equip you to prepare for, manage, mitigate, and influence to the extent that we are able. I hope that you take away from this the important role that your career development plan, professional brand, and self-advocacy plays in your career, as well as how critical it is for you to be able to understand and mitigate biases and how leveraging your voice and influence to do. Regardless of your personal generation, know that in business you will be charged with working with (and sometimes for) persons across multiple backgrounds and generations. The better you are at leading with empathy, being open-minded, and refraining from passing judgement on others based on their perceived place in the journey, the more likely you are to find success for your enterprise and for yourself.

Managing Expectations as a Woman in the Workforce
(*Or, Being a Woman at a Table with Seats Created for Men*)

As a professional working woman, another hurdle that I have had to overcome were the expectations that were placed on me by based on the fact that I am a woman. At times these expectations were direct and other times subtle assumptions about what it means to be a woman navigating a professional environment. It could be anything from the pressure or expectation to overwork if you are a single young professional. There was sometimes an assumption that if you are not openly attached to something or someone other than yourself then you have all this free time and that life is easier.

There were times when I felt an internal and external pressure or expectation to choose between doing something for myself (like visiting with family and spending time engaging in my hobbies) or overworking my way up the corporate ladder. At the same time, I have also observed women who were married and/or did have children who have shared a similar pressure where they were faced with balancing work priorities and family responsibilities. I have heard working mothers vocalize dealing with these subtle assumptions about their ability to meet the job requirements due to the fact that they had a family.

Ultimately, it boiled down to finding what it meant to me to be successful as a woman and what were my expectations for finding an organization, team, colleagues that aligned with this. As a woman who is building a business of her own, know that company culture will be an important factor for you as you decide where and how to embark on this journey - especially if you are creating careers that women could potentially fill. The above are considerations that are on the brains of many women as they are thinking about where they want to work. Fostering an inclusive culture that will attract and retain women will be a more probable outcome for you when you are taking these things into consideration. If you need more support in this area, do not hesitate to check out one of my programs online.

Embracing the Skin that Makes You Authentically Beautiful

(Being and Supporting Women of Color in a World with Basic Check Boxes)

Women of Color are multifaceted and multi-dimensional, yet we are expected to fit in one or two check boxes. You know - the ones that you are asked to fill out in job applications or demographic surveys. For some reasons these boxes are expected to somehow encapsulate all that it means to be woman or minority. There is so much more to us than that. One of my greatest challenges in life, career, and in business is that I do not fit in people's boxes. I stand out - from the color of skin to the tone of my pitch - I stand out. I am a Woman of Color. I am the descendent of slaves who had to overcome, persevere, innovate, survive and thrive against the odds. I do not fit in basic boxes. My personality cannot quite be described but only experienced. No one woman or minority is alike. We are shaped by our unique experiences. We may share commonalities, but we are not the same. Yet we are expected to be/look/sound the same so as to not acknowledge and honor the very things that make us unique and beautiful.

According Glassdoor research, employees who have positive experiences share this with three friends, while those who have negative experiences share it with thousands. This is why it is so important to ensure that employee experiences are measured and analyzed across multiple factors. Though I have had more positive experiences and I share and appreciate those, I can still recall the less than pleasant experiences that absolutely stand out.

For instance, I will never forget the first time I began experimenting with my natural hair. I went to work and I could feel it in my body - the blank stares, the awkward silence, and the desperate and obvious attempts not to stare too hard. It made me uncomfortable, and had a lasting impact on my relationships with my colleagues. This is the kind of conscious and unconscious bias that can impact an employees' experience, an employer's brand, as well as the company culture. It is important to educate yourself, empower yourself with self-advocacy tools, and foster an engaged and inclusive workplace where every employee including minorities feel as though they can bring their whole self (not parts of themselves) to work.

In case you are wondering, currently, I am leveraging tools that empower me to lead more authentically. Now, whether I am wearing my natural or straight hair, I choose to bring my entire self rather than shrink back in discomfort. I encourage you to do the same. Instead of focusing on spaces that make me feel as though my natural hair is unprofessional, I am drawn to spaces where people see it as an extension of my cool, creative, witty , sometimes introverted, very professional when the time calls for it, fun, bubbly, and **outgoing personality**.

Finally, be encouraged on this journey. Sometimes we receive unbalanced feedback that progress is occurring more slowly or not at all. It really depends on who you align yourself with and where you are concentrating your efforts. Be strategic about where you invest your resources and where you align yourself. I have seen and benefited from organizations and individuals who are making strides in these areas, and continue to encourage and support this growth wherever possible.

RECAP & RESOURCES

1. **Manage Your Mindset, and Make Yourself Your First Job** – For more help on this, feel free to check out upcoming Masterclasses.

2. **Know What You Want to Grow** - Develop the self-awareness to know what to prioritize and develop within yourself, your career, and your business through Leadership Development and Employee Engagement assessments. For more help on this, download a free guide on my website and set up a consultation.

3. **Evaluate what You Want to Elevate** - Understand the gap between where you are and what you want to be in terms of a more simplified life or reaching your next career and business goal. An example of this may be you wanting to better understand yourself and your team and so you leverage people technology tools that allow you to better understand your leadership style or employee engagement. For more support on this, book a consultation.

4.

Dictate Your Terms

Alysha M. Campbell

Alysha M. Campbell is an accomplished and respected Strategic HR Leader with a decade of experience that encompasses all facets of Human Resource Management. From executing successful multi-million dollar workforce recruitment and optimization projects to spearheading diverse, equitable, and inclusive employee initiatives, Alysha has truly seen and done it all in the HR space. Her passion for the industry has led her to start her own HR Consultancy and Strategy agency - CultureShift HR.

As Founder of CultureShift HR, Alysha uses her business acumen to help companies utilize and engage their best talent while creating purposeful, diverse, and inclusive work environments that help businesses grow and thrive. Within Alysha's business practices, she encourages companies to embrace the "Employee First" philosophy that focuses on shifting the cultural dynamics and encouraging recognition of positive results and behaviors. Ultimately this leads to greater employee engagement, customer service, and recurring revenue allowing clients to stay competitive in their respective industry and labor market.

Connect with Alysha:
Instagram: https://www.instagram.com/alysha.m.campbell/
Linkedin: https://www.linkedin.com/in/alyshamcampbell/
Twitter: https://twitter.com/AlyshaMCampbell
Email: alysha@cultureshifthr.com
Website: www.cultureshifthr.com
Website: www.alyshacampbell.com

Chapter Eleven:
Finding Balance and Establishing Boundaries – A Recipe for Success
Alysha M. Campbell

Employers are like boyfriends. They want you all to themselves, and when they see you talking to someone else, they get jealous and interfere by reinforcing their own relationship. You can talk about how you want things to be better – earn a higher salary, gain a promotion, aim for further growth – and they'll sweet-talk you and make lofty promises. But sometimes, those promises don't come through and you're left feeling disappointed and unfulfilled. This has been my exact experience with the companies I've worked with; all talk and no change. So when it came to me starting CultureShift HR, I definitely wasn't going to let them or anyone come in and rain on my parade.

To me, CultureShift HR wasn't just a business; it was my stance, the position of my journey of getting out of my 9-5 and creating the life that I wanted. I was exhausted and tired of working twice as hard for half the pay, overlooked for one opportunity after another, my only reprieve being to start at another company and go through the same experience all over again. I was over it. I was done. I wish I could say that I stormed into my boss's office, told them off, stormed back out, and started on my beautiful entrepreneurship journey, but that wasn't the case. I had to play it safe, as I still needed my 9-5 to help me build this new business. I didn't want to start my business with debt and get a loan to fund its fundamentals. As often as you see posts of entrepreneurs living on yachts, eating caviar three times a week, and working from exotic places all over the world, that isn't reality – at least, not mine. Slowly, I started to outline what I wanted CultureShift HR to be and how I was going to make this dream my reality. Piece by piece, elements of the business began to come together. From choosing the name and getting my logo made to identifying the services I was going to offer, watching everything come to life was scary but exciting at the same time. I approached building my business like raising a child; with love, care, and lots of attention. For example, during my working day on my lunch break or during a lull period, I would research, plan, and create the framework. Not a day went by that I didn't think, talk, or do something in service to my business. It was my top priority, and those closest to me knew it and supported me 100%.

Finding Balance in Self-Validation

Finding the energy to build my own business while still employed full time was not an easy task. When I started this venture, I needed to look at how I managed my time, but also at how I lived my life. I needed to ensure I was getting the rest, nutrition, and mental clarity necessary to be my best in the evening hours. Was I just gallivanting around, or was I researching new ideas? Was I surrounding myself by naysayers who didn't see the vision I was trying to create and were draining all my energy, or by those who uplifted me and fueled me to be my best? As I began to change elements of my life to take on this new venture, doing double duty became easier and more manageable. One surprising thing was that getting my dose of creativity and fulfillment from CultureShift HR allowed me to enjoy elements of day job a little more. I had more hope, more resilience, because I knew my future wasn't going to be stuck between those four walls forever; one day, I would be free to be fully engaged in this fantastic business I was building, and the prospect of that made everything more tolerable.

What's interesting is that when starting something from nothing, you learn a lot about yourself in the process – things that I maybe wouldn't need to know if not for beginning my business. The biggest lesson I've learned, and what I continue to learn every day, is to trust myself and my instinct. See, for me, I craved validation from my managers. I was always looking for that "Great job, Alysha!" or "Well done!" I needed that praise to know I was on the right track and that my work would be rewarded. That's one thing school does terribly wrong; they let you believe that if you study hard, get straight As, and do all those extracurricular activities, you will be recognized and rewarded with great opportunities ahead. That's a lie – straight BS. You could be doing a killer job in your position; making your boss look amazing, continuing to deliver, and going above and beyond what's expected of you. You could be working long hours and taking on double your workload, sacrificing your nights, weekends, and vacations in hopes that it will get you to the next level. And sometimes it does, but more often than not, it doesn't. You continue to get all the work but none of the reward. I was done with that. Slowly, through building my business, I've learned that the only person I need to please is myself. Not in a selfish way, where the only thing that matters is what I want, but in a way that confirms that I don't need anyone's acceptance, validation, or praise to prove that my idea, method, and business are good. If I see that it's good, it's good. There's such freedom and liberty in this mindset that I wouldn't trade it for anything in the world.

As I continued to build CultureShift HR, there were definitely both high and low moments. Whenever I got a new project or client, I was over the moon. To know that they could have gone with any HR consultancy but chose to go with mine made me feel like I won the lottery. Sometimes these types of wins would come fast and furious, but other times, not so much. Many days, I felt that CultureShift HR was in a drought. No one accepted my proposals, I wasn't getting any inbound requests, and the sting of rejection became all too familiar. When times like this happen, it's easy to throw in the towel; to say, "Forget it, I'm just going to work corporate" and call it a day. But my desire and sheer will to see my business thrive, to see me be more than what I saw staring back from the mirror, was strong enough for me to keep pushing and keep fighting for my vision. In life, you aren't born with a cheerleading squad supporting you and cheering you on when the chips are down. You need to be your own damn cheerleader, so that's what I became. I read affirmations, studied books and articles on the power of vision boards and goal-setting, and knew that as long as I didn't give up on myself, I would eventually make it. Were there days I didn't even want to get out of bed? Absolutely. Were there days I didn't know what the heck I was doing and thought I was just going around in circles? Yes! That's the journey of entrepreneurship. If it was easy, everyone would do it (but they don't).

The Fork in the Road

Eventually, there came a point in my journey when I knew I would need to talk to my job about my business. Until this time, I hadn't even put it on my LinkedIn account because I was so afraid it would get me fired from my corporate job. However, if I wanted to take my business to the next level, I knew I now needed to produce content and share who I was and what I was doing. It was a risk. I could put myself out there and my company might not care two cents, or they could be really annoyed and feel that I wasn't a team player.

I had to make a choice. Was my corporate job worth more to me than the business I was building? Was it more to me than the person I was becoming and who I still wanted to be? Was it worth more than my dream? The answer came to me over and over again: no. I was worth more than their salary. I was worth more than my corporate position or label.

From that moment, the decision was easy. However, I didn't tell people directly about CultureShift HR; I showed them. Using the mighty power of social media, I began posting my panel talks, my blogs, my client testimonials, and my brand content – and within two weeks, word got around and the higher-ups started to notice. It was a ballsy move. I wasn't asking for permission; I wasn't coloring within the lines. I was the CEO and Founder of CultureShift HR. I was the one-woman show supporting non-profits, tech businesses, and marketing companies to create diverse, equitable, and inclusive workplaces, and I wasn't going to apologize for it.

To ensure the utmost professionalism, I made every effort to keep CultureShift HR completely separate from my 9-5. This was to show there were not conflicts of interests and no lines blurred. Even if I was offered support or opportunities, I always had to ask myself if this could put the business at risk. If there was any hint of that possibility, no matter how good, I had to say no. And trust me, they came from all sides. But remember, not everything that glitters is gold. In the world of business, endeavors and startups come and go for a variety of reasons. I wanted to ensure my hard work, effort and time had every chance of success possible. Making calculated decisions for the business to ensure it's positioned in the best way possible can be tricky which is why due diligence is key. I found when these opportunities came, what helped guide me in the right direction was remembering and understanding who I was transforming into. I wasn't just Alysha the employee; I was Alysha M. Campbell, the CEO and Founder of CultureShift HR, and no one was going to short cut my success by piggyback on my hard work and long nights. Being able to achieve what I have, although small but mighty, meant more to me than I knew. It took me from relying on others' opinions and validations to not needing or caring about it at all. That right there is my super power and it's priceless.

Lessons Learned Along the Way

As CultureShift HR grew, it became more and more vital to ensure my environment and surroundings were set up for success. Jiving with the right pace, being in the mental space, and obtaining the flexibility to continue exploring became my focus. As I've continued on this journey, I've come to fully realize that I don't need to settle for anything I don't want. If you want something, go after it and get it. You need to know and understand your worth before you can expect anyone else to, or else you'll be constantly standing in someone else's shadow. Don't. Learn to appreciate, congratulate, and love who you are and what you're doing, because no one else will in the way you require.

I've also since learned that these lessons are only the beginning. This journey has only just begun. I am beyond excited for the future of CultureShift HR, and I know it will be so much more than I've ever imagined. I know that I have plenty more growing to do, but I'm getting there every day. Most of all, I know that I'm enough, and completely worthy of all the success that comes my way.

Jessica Canty

Jessica Canty is a life and career strategist specializing in helping Melanin Millennial Moms go from unfulfilling jobs to their dream careers. With more than 20 years of experience in the career coaching industry, Jessica employs unique and engaging strategies for supporting her clients in achieving their career goals.

Jessica is the creator of the innovative and insightful "Work Journal: A Place to Develop How Awesome You Are" which utilizes over 100 hours of career coaching tools based on Jessica's own trademark Canty Model of Career Development to support her followers in their continued career development. She is also a recurring personality featured on SwagHer magazine where she regularly contributes career and lifestyle advice to readers.

Connect with Jessica:

Website: https://www.jessicacanty.com/
Facebook: https://www.facebook.com/groups/307429470280711/
LinkedIn: https://www.linkedin.com/in/jessica-canty-licsw-86973231/
Instagram: https://www.instagram.com/jessicacanty/
Twitter: https://twitter.com/jessicacanty8

To read more from Jessica, check out her contributions to SwagHer Magazine here:
https://swagheronline.com/?s=jessica+canty

Chapter Twelve: Building Up and Breaking Through - Overcoming Setbacks and Positioning Myself for Success
Jessica Canty

If you have seen any of my material via social media, my services, or products, you know that I have a mission to support melanin millennial moms who want high achieving careers. I wish I could say that my mission came to me in dream, or that a moment of inspiration hit me during my morning coffee, but that simply isn't my story. The mission of my company was birthed out of devastation, divorce, and death, and ultimately devotion. The lessons that I learned from those experiences established the framework that I created to get myself a $30k raise, coach clients into promotions, and has made me a sought-after speaker. I'm going to share with you the pitfalls that I fell into to help you avoid them and fast-track your unique brand of success.

The Burn-Out

I was miserable in what was supposed to be my dream career. I spent six years pursuing two collegiate degrees and was thousands of dollars in debt for a profession I was once passionate about. The dreams I pursued became what made me dread Monday mornings. My salary was dismal, and I can recall having to look between couch cushions to find money to go to the grocery store for my young family. I felt overwhelmed, unseen, and stuck. I struggled to pay my rent or buy diapers for my daughter. I even remember having to call out of work at one point because I couldn't afford the gas to get there! I was tired of being tired - I knew something had to change. I just didn't know where to start.

I tried and tested a litany of ideas for fixing my financial issues. From couponing to spending freezes and even misguided attempts at part time employment – it seemed like at some point I had tried it all. And yet, I still found myself with a negative bank account at the end of the month. Sis, life was hard!! If you are experiencing hard times that seem unsurmountable, please know that success is still your destiny.

You are incredibly skilled and designed to create unique solutions for your clients and companies. Your devastations are pitfalls that can be leveraged for your next best business move. Your value is not in being overlooked for a promotion or having trained your replacement. Your value is in how your education, emotions, and experiences are packaged and performed by you. No one can do what you do the way you do it. You are capable of turning your pitfalls into profits, and I'm going to tell you how:

Mindset Shift: Your Purpose and Profit are in Your Pain.

When you feel like you have had too many setbacks to be a success, it's time to apply this mindset shift. Applying this mindset shift will help you make the power move below. Start by writing a list of the challenges you have overcome – what are your successes? What things have you accomplished that you are proud of? Bring that list to your work to guide you when you're ready to start the next step.

Your *career niche and branding* are built from the success framework that you learned to overcome your challenges. Think about those challenges, and how you've been able to persevere. This will tell you a lot about yourself and help you move further forward toward success.

Sometimes, even when we are working toward our own success, we get stuck along the way. We stop believing in ourselves and our ability to do things. When that happens, I recommend employing affirmations to help get you back on track. Affirmations are defined as formal declarations of support or encouragement. We often give affirmations to others through praise for their good work, but they can be especially useful for encouraging and affirming ourselves, as well. Use this tool to give you confidence when you feel overwhelmed with life's challenges.

Composing affirmations can seem a little strange at first, if you aren't accustomed to the practice. However, they are relatively easy to compose and can definitely make a difference in the way you view yourself and your work. Below are a few to get you started:

I will have all the resources I need to do transformational work.

I will earn the salary that will provide for the lifestyle I desire.

I am excited about the work I do.

My clients know that I diligently work to be a reliable source for their unmet needs.

Opportunity chases me down.

People develop opportunities to meet my talent.

My career executive board is my success squad, and they have the mission to see me successful in my business and career endeavors.

All my communication will reflect that I am a subject matter expert.

I can and do love working.

Dreams Denied, Devastation Realized

For as long as I can remember, I have dreamt of being a wife and mother. For my sixth birthday, I even recall asking my parents to get me a bride costume. As I grew into adulthood, I purposely positioned myself to become the ultimate wife with my homemaking skills, empathy muscles, financial stability, and even in my grooming practices. So, you can imagine my elation when I was asked to marry the man that I had determined would be my husband from the moment I saw him. When I said "I do," however, I had no idea what was in store for me.

There were good times and successes in my marriage, particularly in the beginning. Unfortunately, the sweet spots were outnumbered by the storms, and my husband and I eventually decided that life was not a journey we were meant to pursue together. When my marriage ended in divorce, I felt deflated and unworthy. I was reeling from the hurt I experienced in it and that hurt was compounded by the grief we experienced when we lost our youngest daughter.

Faced with an unexpected amount of pain that no woman should have to endure, I decided to channel my hurt and healing into something positive. My pain made clear where my focus should be, and helped me define my niche – really, my purpose – in working to support the development and growth of other melanin millennial moms like me, who just needed a win. I utilized this new skillset that I hadn't even realized I'd been developing to lead and counsel with empathy mothers from all sorts of backgrounds, going through a multitude of changes in their lives. Expecting mothers, grieving mothers, married and unmarried mothers, even abused and neglected mothers - I am especially grateful that my challenges have positioned me in a way that allows me to support them all in realizing their dreams and creating full lives for themselves.

Mindset Shift: The Best Is Yet to Come!

When all your goals are experiencing turmoil and you don't see a way out, remember that you are deserving of the best that life has to offer. Your best is coming to you because it was designed for you. One great strategy for staying on trach is to set **"Wellbeing Checkpoints"** along the way and write your own **"Vision of Success."**

Solidifying your place in your dream career takes more than networking, resume changes, and office dos and don'ts. You must be a good steward over the tools and resources assigned to you and prioritize maintaining the most important tool. (**Hint...Hint... the most important tool is <u>you</u>!**) The concept of career wellbeing is a systematic way of implementing maintenance of the different aspects that create a balance in your workplace. Doing this regularly is vital to your longevity in any given profession – whether you're working for yourself or for someone else. As a rule of thumb, you should assess your career wellbeing monthly, thinking critically about the different things that factor into your business on a daily basis. This can include your work environment, the amount of time that you devote to your tasks, how effective you feel that your business is at reaching your mission, the amount of monetary return you're generating on your time and energy investment, etc.

Write these factors down on a sheet of paper, spelling out the top categories that are most important to you in your career and business. Then, rate each element on a scale of 1-5, 1 being "poor" and 5 being "excellent." When you rate each element ask yourself: Why did I score it this way? What would increase the score? What would maintain the score? How has the score impacted me personally? If you find that you are seeing a decline in your personal wellbeing, assess for any connection in the way you score for your career wellbeing.

Next, you'll want to take a moment and create what I like to call a "Career Visualization Board." I've learned through many years of coaching that most people can clearly explain what they don't want from their career, but they sometimes have trouble articulating the things that they **DO** want. In detail, they can tell you what salary they won't accept, schedule they refuse to work, or responsibilities they don't feel comfortable fulfilling. While this is all well and good when working for others, the concept becomes a little less clear when we consider our own business endeavors. We tend to be less comfortable with establishing boundaries and stating outright what we need or expect from our own businesses, which in turn leads to many people becoming less than successful in their entrepreneurial endeavors.

To assess if the current trajectory of your business meets the requirements to be deemed your dream career, you must know what you do want along with what you don't want. This tool is designed to be a space to visualize what you want from and for your career. Take a moment to think about how you want to feel as the owner of your own enterprise. Visualize what you want in your salary and what you will do with it. Once you have visualized it, it's critical to see it physically, and to see it often. I encourage you to, on a sheet of paper, create a matrix similar to the one below. In the spaces of your matrix, place or draw pictures, words, quotes, phrases that reflect the career you want to build through your business.

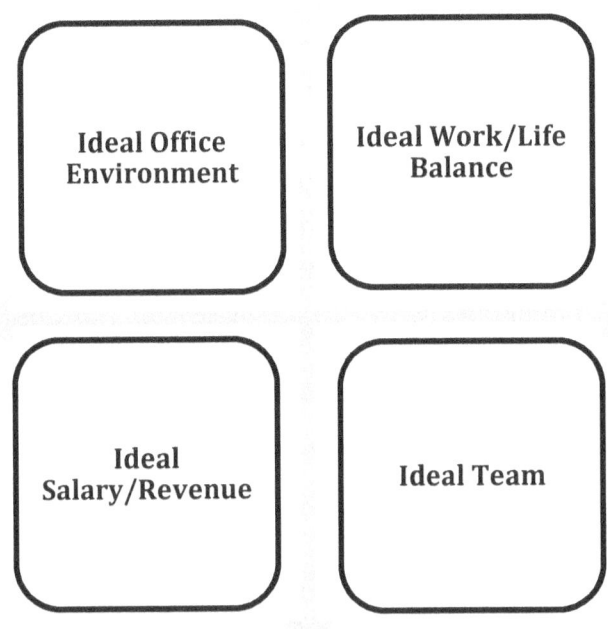

Once you've created your vision board, be sure not to simply put it away somewhere and forget about it. Put this career visualization board in a prominent place in your home or office – somewhere that you will see often. Bring it out whenever you apply for a job, interview with a potential client, or when you meet with your executive board. Having the visual close will encourage you and give you the momentum you need in moments of low energy and motivation.

Building Your Board – Level Up with Your Career Success Squad

I have been devastated by getting passed up for a promotion I thought I was overly qualified for. I have experienced the frustration of not hearing back from companies that I thought I interviewed well for. I still have the worry lines under my eyes left from the countless hours I spent posting resumes for jobs that I never heard back from. I am embarrassed to say that I accepted low ball salary offers for too many jobs. I did not know how to brand myself and did not know how to learn to. I saw others living the success that I felt was slowly slipping away from me. That reality does not have to be your own.

Mindset Shift: Make Executive-Level Decisions with Your Career

One of the most important things I finally learned was to *fast-track my own success by learning from the trials of others.* You do this by networking and researching industry professionals who are willing to invest in you. Don't leave the power of your career success and happiness in the hands of clients and companies. YOU have the agency and authority to create your ideal life and career on your own terms. You only need to take hold of that agency and harness it to build the business that serves your needs and allows you to make the impact that you want to have on the world.

When I started this business, I had family tell me that I was not being a good mother by having two jobs. I heard that I was neglecting my daughter and not being a Biblical mother. The words hurt and I was racked with mommy guilt. That all changed when I realized that by having a business, I was giving my daughter permission to pursue her goals. My motivation is to build a tribe of women who show their daughters they can be a mom, mogul, employee, and even the Vice President of the United States of America!

You must believe that are not less than others because they have achieved the success that you have yet to. Just because you may still be in the process of becoming the businesswoman that you want to be does not mean that you are less worthy of the things that your heart and mind desire. You are fully capable of birthing a successful business, of creating a fulfilling life in and outside of work, and of making an impact on the world.

Further, you need to surround yourself with people who see that value and promise in you as well. Often our families – those that in theory should be the ones to support us no matter what – are the very same people who are skeptical and critical of moves that we make toward our success. It is important that you have the right people in your life – those who can accompany you on your journey and who can be cheerleaders and accountability partners along the way, mentoring you into the best version of yourself and your business.

Here is where I underscore the importance of building your career success squad. Think of these people as your personal board of directors. They are the ones who will shine a light on your strengths (and weaknesses) and help guide you forward in the best way possible. In general, your success squad should include someone who fits into each of the following categories:

Role Model: Choose a person who is successful in the profession and lifestyle you want for yourself. Your role model can be admired and emulated from afar and you do not need to know them personally.

Mentor: Chose a person who is available and willing to share their success strategies with at least twice a month.

Coach: A coach will help you map out the path towards the career you want. They should be a good fit for your unique career challenges and have a proven track record of getting clients success.

Sponsor: A sponsor will leverage their influence and power to connect you with industry insiders and potential funders.

Mindset Shift: Slow Progress is Still Progress.

My whole life I've always had external voices telling me how I didn't qualify or was not the right fit. In my childhood I was called "goody two shoes"," teacher's pet", and "book smart, not street smart." As a teenager I was an outcast for not having trendy clothing and limited social interactions. As an adult I was "too fat", "not Black/ Christian enough", "nappy headed", and "poorly educated…what can an HBCU teach you?"

All those external voices became my internal gauge of my worthiness for success. It set the stage for me to have a seemingly incurable case of imposter syndrome. I had to find a way to reset my mental frameworks or succumb to a life of monotony and complacency. When you feel overwhelmed or anxious about having to balancing your tight budget and messy bookbags, laundry and long list of homework, all while showing up in your work, take a look back at that list of accomplishments you made earlier. Remind yourself that you are successful, that you are capable of accomplishing great things, and that the best is yet to come for you.

You deserve every good thing that comes your way and more – but it is up to you to go out and make your dreams happen. As Black women, we learn early that no one is going to "give" us anything – we dream it, we work hard, and we realize those dreams one by one. Remember that, no matter where you are in your journey, it is not too late. You are not too lost. You are exactly where you need to be in this moment, and you have all the tools necessary to achieve those dreams in your business and in life.

Good luck, sis – I'm rooting for you!

Dee Burrowes

Dee Burrowes is a Certified Professional Coach, NLP Practitioner, and Speaker who helps women to shift from a state of uncertainty, self-doubt and comparison syndrome to guiding into their greatness of more confidence, to radical self-belief, happiness and feeling worthy. She has been featured in multiple print and online publications both in the United Kingdom and internationally. Dee is continuously on a mission to share her journey and fully understands how to excel in a career culture, embracing diversity and change.

Connect with Dee:

LinkedIn: https://www.linkedin.com/in/mindsetstrategist
Instagram: https://www.instagram.com/dee_burrowes/
Facebook: https://www.facebook.com/deeburrowescoach
Website: www.AchievePureBrilliance.com

Chapter Thirteen: Winning From Within
Dee Burrowes

Let me tell you a secret: there is no limit to our potential - absolutely none, despite the many excuses that we dish out on a daily basis. At times however, we may be guilty of getting in our own way. Too often we play it safe, barely taking the necessary steps to move forward, refusing to go into the deep. We cling to the shallowest end in the pool of our subconscious, purposely ignoring anything that might challenge (and thus scare) us.

In order to realize my dreams, I had to strategically harness tools and tack. I had to make the conscious decision to move forward, away from expectations engrained in me by family, culture, and society and trust in the process of transformation as I worked to pave a path of my own. Through hard work, dedication, a touch of gusto, and just a bit of blessings along the way, I successfully moved through the challenges set before me and built a life and business that I so richly deserve.

From a humble, yet stable beginning I have been able to birth great achievements. Along the way, there has been a great deal of learning and growing as a result of the obstacles thrown in my path. I grew up an only child, spending most of my childhood in Kingston, Jamaica prior to immigrating to the United Kingdom in early adulthood. From the beginning, I was expected to do well and succeed at my endeavours. Driven by this motivation, I was eager to go to school and excel at academia. This ambition has continued to motivate me well into adulthood, and even now I am an overachiever – a go-getter, a warrior, a lioness and a strong woman. I am fortunate to have a mother who was deliberate in forging a better life for me than the one she had. She worked very hard across a few streams of income to provide for all that I needed. In reward for her hard work I became steadfast in my determination to capitalize on the opportunities that I was presented. Far from being the spoiled child, it might seem to some that the odds were stacked against me in the beginning. Luckily, I was raised by a mother who was a firm believer in compassion and discipline. As I grew into an adult, this background supported my burgeoning confidence, independence and leadership.

I have also faced marginalization as a Brown-skinned girl in modern Britain. I have worked thrice as hard as my non-Brown counterparts for even a bit of access to the infamous "table", and even harder in earning a seat to enjoy a cuppa and scones. Once I achieved my seat, I remember being told that I should be grateful for the privilege, as many times I have been the only Brown person there. Instead, I use this as a catalyst to continue with my pre-ordained goals, climbing higher still. In one of the many poignant moments in my personal and professional life, I have come to recognize that it is not the table that defines my success, but rather it is my support system and inner will to overcome the barriers that have shaped me into the woman I am today.

By refusing to be disregarded and overlooked, I've given rise to my own brilliance and strength, embarking on a journey to new and fascinating heights. I stand before you now an acclaimed speaker, author, columnist, mindset coach, and professor. I avail to others the testimony of my triumph, victory and self-transformation and encourage others to rebuild emotional, mental, financial and spiritual connectedness for the same. Mine is a story that may be similar to your journey. I have been fortunate to build a career spanning more than two decades as a 9-5er in the hospitality industry, including roles in accounting and education, and I now operate a life coaching mental health practice where I facilitate individuals unfolding and blooming into their highest selves and achieving a life of fulfilment.

I've learned along the way one great truth: mindset is everything. It does not matter how skilled, talented, or connected you are. If you have not crafted the right mindset, you will never achieve your desired dreams and aspirations. The mindset you cultivate, and how you use it to your benefit, will determine where you meet success or your own demise.

As I figured out life and began cultivating a winning mindset, I had to reframe and relearn what I was taught through my environment and professional culture. My sweat was entrenched between the bricks of these corporate companies I had worked for. I worked hard, strived for perfection and many times committed to a company or cause as though it was my own name on the establishment, instead of my superiors. Eventually, however, I grew tired of that and went in search of something more. Through intentional personal development, I uncovered my reason for being – my *ikigai*. I had a focus with an intensity few can realize as I worked to reprogram my mindset. I read books and articles, watched seminars, and did my best to learn and model the success I saw in others. Along the way, I developed what I see as my personal approach to the mindset shift, outlined for you here.

The Self-Care Approach

I welcome the idea of prioritizing self-care, using my voice for change and being the best version of myself - unapologetically. Often times our commitment to our own self-care gets off course amidst the hustle and bustle of everyday life. Distractions like our mobile phones, family commitments, a stressful career and other ever looming tasks needing attention almost immediately can force us to make hard choices about what we "must do"... many times leading to the neglect of ourselves as we are pushed further and further down the list. It seems as though something always comes up, taking precedence over our own care and resulting in us somehow multitasking, juggling everything all at once.

In reality, there is power in granting yourself permission to do nothing without any expectancy. I am a firm believer that self-care should not be perceived as an escape from your life. It must be a regular and consistent part of your lifestyle incorporating routines and habits fueling small, gradual changes in looking after yourself. It's time to overhaul your mind, spirit, body and once this occurs, you will be unstoppable.

This isn't a change that happens all at once, though. I strive daily to make healthier choices, and have found that implementing the following self-care tips intentionally and regularly, I've been much more successful in my overall cultivation of this mindset and lifestyle:

1. Laugh plenty - humor is fun and free.
2. Be kind to yourself and others.
3. Activate all of your senses, especially touch. Indulge in a facial and body massage to elevate your mood and lift your spirits.
4. Choose to say "No" without the guilty emotions – cease the people-pleasing.
5. Check in with your thoughts and words often - they become your actions.
6. Wake up early with intention and a well-committed morning routine.
7. Set healthy boundaries and be unapologetic about enforcing them.

For years I have struggled with people-pleasing, how to obtain a fulfilled and content life ceasing any form of status quo or societal norms. But I've learned that that's no way to live your best authentic life. A matter of fact, life is just about unravelling your world to new possibilities - the adventures, the taking the step without envisioning the entire staircase and being proud of yourself.

After missed opportunities for promotion, working in toxic environment and experiencing racism within a certain professional body sphere, I began exploring a new way to achieve success on my own terms. I have now been able to carry the torch and the lights have now been sparked with in me. I am on fire and the flames are burning within my soul. I had felt stifled and frustrated, a far cry from life as it is now – rife with accomplishment, growth, believe, fulfilment and harmony.

I've learned in life and similarly in business, there will be many obstacles blocking the way of your destiny. Learning to let go and accept the power of forgiveness is one critical measure in crafting success on your own terms. Life is seldom as perfect as people let on. Adversity and difficult times are a part of everyone's life. How you bounce back from these challenges is what really defines you. It is your tool box of resilience and mindset which governs your happiness and willpower. For every mistake, there's a golden egg of opportunities waiting on the other side of the struggles. In all honestly, there were times when the obstacles were a sign of failure and I felt discouraged and overwhelmed with negative emotions that no doubt weakened my ability and motivation to work toward achieving my goals. These emotions could potentially dissuade you from attempting to overcome the obstacle even as you know it is the right thing to do. The key is not to surrender without considering a solution to the obstacle and your emotional reaction to such.

In fact, it can be proven how quickly you can turn around even the most negative of situations with support and the right mindset. What will your spark look like?

I have enthusiastically dreamt of a lifestyle that having best of this world in the sunshine, but I had several times dismissed the idea as I thought I was bound to a professional networking body that never valued my skills and talents. Somewhere along the way I divested myself from that negative thinking and created my own meaning of success. And that dream? I began to bring it to life even in a season where most are uncertain of their next move. For the past few months, I decided to forego my traditional living arrangements and embark on the nomadic professional lifestyle. I am currently living the laptop life, working remotely from some of my favorite locations. I have a lush place I call home, peace of mind, a tribe of influence, and am walking amongst Kings, Queens, Heads of States while making a profound global impact changing lives one by one as I learn and grow myself.

Starting my own business was no easy feat. When you've thought the corporate table has served you well, despite not being seated to eat an enjoyable meal amongst those who were given the chance to, it can be daunting to move away from that into the unknown. Still, I had faith after planting the seed for my new beginning. I have nurtured it and watched it grow - now its harvest time.

I encourage you to invest time in evaluating how you can be a more authentic form of yourself. Honour your struggles and consciously cultivate increased alignment and genuineness in yourself. The opportunity to grow and be will be inevitable as you walk away from rejection into your miracle with your head held high. A winning mindset is the idea that your qualities can cultivate positive change and growth through your intentional efforts.

It's likely why we tend to feel more stung by rejection and mishaps even by failure as it will open the door to opportunities, abundance, and freedom.

I am the kind of woman who sees light, beauty, pain, power and shame in everything almost simultaneously.

I am the kind of woman who refuses to be fearful, petrified, and scared.

I've been able to truly feel my force – my energy – and recognise and harness my power.

We all need a little inspiration from time to time, and if you know where to search for it, you will find yourself on the brighter side before you know it. Go ahead and find it.

It has been the greatest gift of finding my power finally – I have no profound regrets of the journey. Living life in a cubicle bubble is no way to live; life's about opening up your world to new experiences! It's about adventure, even in the smallest form of the word.

Stay plugged in and focused – carry on and live life to the absolute fullest.

Sydney Davis

Sydney is the founder of Tequity, a SaaS company that provides app development services and support to underrepresented and underserved entrepreneurs. With over a decade of entrepreneurship and tech experience, Sydney encourages diversity of thought among community leaders to partner to provide accessible and affordable app and web development software for those of any technical ability.

She is an activist for removing barriers for marginalized people in the tech, arts & startup industries through software development & coaching. She is an Executive Director & Entrepreneur with over 10 years of software, web & app development and project management experience. Sydney is notable for developing over 250 apps for tech startups and has won numerous pitch competitions.

Connect with Sydney:

LinkedIn: https://www.linkedin.com/in/iamsydneydavis/
Twitter: https://twitter.com/Iammisslorraine
Website: https://www.sydneylorraine.com/
Website: https://www.tequityapps.com/

Chapter Fourteen: Wearing Two Hats - Transparency and Authenticity as an Employed Entrepreneur
Sydney Davis

I started my entrepreneurship journey long before I accepted my first corporate job. I began as a freelance web developer in undergrad, working throughout college to help fund my education. Upon graduation, I continued freelancing, balancing my business and honing my skills while also embarking on my first full-time, professional job. I had established a great working relationship with my boss at the time. She was a Black woman from Ohio who just seemed to have it all, engineering degree, vast work experience, and she was in leadership. She quickly took me under her wing as my mentor, and was genuinely invested in my overall professional development. As a brand new college grad finding my way in my first ever corporate work experience, this was a blessing. I was able to be transparent about my goals, and where I saw myself in the future. Entrepreneurship was always something that I was passionate about and intended to continue pursuing, and it was important to me to find opportunities in my day job that complimented my personal professional goals.

Every quarter I would have a goal session with my supervisor, where I had the opportunity to talk about what I wanted to achieve in my role. In preparing for these sessions, I made sure to focus on how the objectives of my role aligned with my personal entrepreneurial goals down the line. Though I was very much committed to doing great work for the company, I also recognized that they benefitted a great deal from having me on staff. While I was more than happy to give my time and talent to my role, I prioritized honing my own skill set, ensuring that I would be able to take with me valuable experience and skills if and when I decided to move on from this organization. I was transparent about this with my mentor, letting her know that, while I was committed to my role within the company, I also had a bigger picture in mind that I was preparing for and working toward. My mentor/supervisor was very supportive of this, opening my mind to ways that I could streamline the work I did in my every day job and identifying key areas of opportunity that would not only make me a better asset for the company, but would also develop me to be a better entrepreneur. For entrepreneurs who are still working a regular job, one key strategy for being successful is to treat your role like you would your own business. Lead and get results the way you would in your own enterprise – this not only builds trust with your employer, but also serves as a good personal discovery practice for yourself and finding your brand style.

You may be thinking, "Well, how am I going to find areas in my job that will support my entrepreneurship?" The truth is, this is easier than you think. Nearly all businesses, no matter how big or small, utilize similar processes in order to achieve success. The biggest difference is that those major companies that hire us simply have more capital to invest in perfecting those processes. While you may not be able to replicate them in your own business (yet), you can still learn what to look for and find ways to implement them on a smaller scale where possible.

The reason that I'm able to be strategic and set key performance metrics for my company, Tequity, is because I've worked in a Fortune 400 company and have seen firsthand how they do it. I've watched as process maps are developed and I've witnessed & assisted in automating department operations. I was able to take certification classes around Change Management through my employer's professional development offerings. Change management is a strategy that corporate executives use when they want to roll out key operational changes and need their employees to buy-in to the new way of doing things. I applied that learning to sales for my own business and discovered how to best communicate my value to leads who are struggling to accept or engage with me. All the time I was working for someone else, I was learning and absorbing critical strategies that I would later apply in my own business.

Sometime, though, we may not have opportunities for continuing professional development. You may need to get creative in how you build skills that will work for you in your business – but remember that it's never impossible. There are always opportunities to hone and build your skill set; but they may look a little different than you expect. For example: if you can't find opportunities in your role that directly relate to your business, then focus on strengthening your skill set as a servant leader. Servant leadership is what makes really great leaders people want to work with and work for.

Servant leadership: a leadership philosophy in which the goal of the leader is to serve.

This is different from traditional leadership where the leader's main focus is the thriving of their company or organization. A servant leader shares power, puts the needs of the employees first, and helps people develop and perform as highly as possible.

Servant leaders are a revolutionary bunch. They take the traditional power leadership model and turn it completely upside down. This new hierarchy puts the people (i.e. – clients… or employees, depending on the context), at the very top of the proverbial pyramid and the leader at the bottom. The leader understands that they are charged with serving those above them - and that's just the way servant leaders like it.

That's because these leaders possess a serve-first mindset, and they are focused on empowering and uplifting those who work for them and who they are working for. They are serving instead of commanding, showing humility instead of brandishing authority, and always looking to enhance the development of others in ways that unlock potential, creativity and sense of purpose. Having this example before me, I was better prepared to lead others, better serve clients and have others work hard for me in my own company.

As I stated previously – I have always been open and transparent about my entrepreneurial endeavors. Everyone in my company knew that I was an entrepreneur on my own time, but I made sure to also be a great employee and deliver excellent results for my clients and my team. I also made sure to keep the two worlds separate, so while my company knew that I was an entrepreneur outside of work hours, I took several steps to ensure that none of my actions could be misconstrued as mixing the two. A few of the strategies that I employed to do this included:

1. - I never did my business work on company time. Now, I may do some side-business work on my lunch break only, but I have always been respectful of the boundaries for my job. This helped to protect me (and my business) by ensuring that there were no blurred lines, and that any resources I utilized in my business were gained fairly and in a legitimate manner.

2. - I was always learning and developing myself through my role. I was able to leverage my 9-5 was building

relationships through my role with external independent consultants. This is something that I recommend to all entrepreneurs, as networking is the bedrock for the success of most any business. Networking authentically allowed me to cultivate connections that I could take with me when I moved on from my role into something else.

3. – I showed up as my best self every day, demonstrating my commitment to my job and getting results that made it clear that I was more than earning my keep.

The key is to continue to think of the big picture. I challenge you to make a list of things you want to achieve, or secure while you're still working in your regular job. When I was working in corporate I made a list during my performance goals sessions with my boss. One of those items on the list was to get my project management degree and certification; not because I was passionate to do project management for them, but I knew I wanted the credentials and I wanted the knowledge so that I could take the skillset into my entrepreneurship. I knew it would be required of me to be an excellent project manager to successfully run a tech company.

So what is it that you want to get accomplished? Is it a degree, a certificate or a training program? What conferences do you want to attend on their budget? Do you want to leave the job at a certain salary? Is there anyone in particular who you want to get closer to in the company to learn about what they do? Begin identifying the things that can apply to your entrepreneurship journey that will benefit you within the job and beyond.

This strategy has been critical to my success, and has even allowed me to move into a different role (this time as Executive Director of a non-profit) while also running my multi-million dollar tech business. I'm offered flexibility and resources to benefit myself, my bigger goals, and the job.

I maintain integrity and trust with my employer by being honest and open about my intentions, so that there is no ambiguity or guesswork involved. I'm committed to the work that I'm doing, meaning I don't miss deadlines, I over deliver and I'm on time. Consistency builds trust, so even more than communication, your actions need to align with your intentions as well. I'm a strong believer that if you're doing the work exceedingly well & above expectations people are more open and receptive to whatever else you do outside of work as long as it doesn't interfere.

Christon Stewart

Christon Stewart is a Detroit native and a single mother who does graphic design day and night. During the day, she works for Rocket Mortgage as a Content Creator (which is a fancy word for graphic designer) and by evening she is the founder and graphic designer of her own business, Twenty One Design and Promotions. Not only does she have a freelance graphic design business, but she also has a few T-shirt lines (and she crafts in her spare time!)

With Christon's passion and skills she has for graphic design, she decided to continue to work full time, all while pursuing an entrepreneurship freelance business. Her beliefs on satisfying her clients are based on what they envision their brand or business to be and how she can bring that to life.

Connect with Christon:

Website, Twenty One Designs: www.twentyonedesigns.com
Website, Twenty One Apparel: www.shoptwentyoneapparel.com
Facebook: https://www.facebook.com/twentyonedesign.promotions
Instagram: https://www.instagram.com/21designandpromotions/
Facebook: https://www.facebook.com/search/top?q=twenty%20one%20apparel
Instagram: https://www.instagram.com/shoptwentyoneapparel/

Chapter Fifteen: Strategy, Balance, and Staying the Course
Christon Stewart

Excuse my French, but how in the absolute F&%# do we do this? This thing they call work/life "balance"? I honestly don't even know how I do it, but I do. I have been in business for seven years and in that time, I have always had a job working somewhere as well. I never understood why a lot of people would say work your 9-5 to fund your business and then eventually quit that 9-5 to go become a full-time entrepreneur. I get that for some people, that may be the best path, but it hasn't been for me. That's not to say that I would **never** want to become a full-time entrepreneur, but I recognize that there are many benefits to remaining gainfully employed, and I want to take advantage of those as I continue to grow my business and my skills.

I'm Christon Stewart, by the way – owner of Twenty One Design and Promotions. I'm a native of Detroit and a graduate of Grand Valley State University, where I studied Advertising and Public Relations. I've always been what I would describe as a creative individual, even from a young age. In high school, I was always the kid you could catch in the yearbook room, editing photos and putting together layouts for that year's edition, or designing graphics for close family and friends. Eventually, people began asking me to help them put together marketing materials for their businesses, which opened my eyes for the first time to the possibility that this design hobby of mine might be a real, viable business opportunity for me.

During my time at Grand Valley State, I was able to explore another realm in the marketing world – advertising, and I quickly fell in love with it. I learned that it wasn't just about designing "pretty things" but designing things that are strategically appealing to specific target audiences and designing things so that the reader can understand what the message is portraying immediately upon seeing it. At the same time, I was running my freelance design business in earnest, creating graphics, social media templates, websites... you name it. The possibilities were endless – I was servicing entrepreneurs and business owners from all around!

As I completed college, I still ran my graphic design business and began focusing on growing and developing my skillset. I wanted to become a better designer, and utilized all the tools at my disposal to do that. YouTube Academy was (and still is) my best friend. In 2014, I decided to formally establish myself as Twenty One Design and Promotions. I worked diligently to improve the look of professionalism in my brand, revamping my website, creating stronger contracts, developing engaging social media content, and even booking a professional photoshoot. I wanted to make sure that I gave my clients the best possible experience when working with me, and that started with giving them professional-level services as soon as they walked through my (virtual) front door.

I also took some time to really think about what kinds of services I wanted my business to offer to my clients, and what the purpose of my business should be. A little fun fact about my business: it is named after my father. I lost my father at the age of 7 and the trauma that can do for a little girl who loved her father so much played a major role in the person I've grown to become. My father's nickname was "Big Daddy 21" or just "21" (he loved black jack and would whoop some ass in a second at the card table). What better way to have my father with me throughout my business? I know that if he was here, he would be supporting me like no other, so I named my business in honor of him.

Through Twenty One Design and Promotions, I offer graphics, branding, and promotional services to entrepreneurs that support them in growing their businesses. Not only do I focus on design concepts, but I also help with promoting their business or brand. I enjoy working with people who are just as excited as I am about building their business and creating a brand for themselves, and have clients that come from a wide variety of industries and backgrounds. From realtors, hairstylists, photographers, authors, churches, media companies, chefs, etc. I enjoy working with a versatile group of clients because it allows me the opportunity to play around with different design elements/concepts, and really stretch myself creatively to deliver a unique and engaging end-product that my clients love.

Because I work with new and aspiring entrepreneurs, I sometimes find myself needing to do a little bit of informal coaching as well. For new business owners who are just getting started, here is the best advice that I have learned over the last several years as an entrepreneur myself:

1. - **Never let anyone tell you soon as you start your business you have to become a full-time entrepreneur and quit your 9-5.** Do it on your terms and when you're ready to, not because someone told you you're not living up to your full potential as an entrepreneur. Full-time entrepreneurship is not for the faint of heart, and especially if you have children or other family depending on you, it is always a good idea to go slowly and work your way into being a solo entrepreneur.

2. - **It's okay to turn that hobby into a business.** If you're passionate about something or simply love what you're doing, make it into something professional. Set up your LLC, trademark, EIN, websites, contracts, and start taking your business seriously - especially if you want others to do the same in return.

3. - **NEVER. GIVE. UP.** - I have doubts every time I am unable to get some things accomplished or my check list completed. Know that not only are you doing this business for yourself, but also for the people who support and work with you. They are the reason you should keep pushing, even when you doubt yourself.

4. - **Never start out on 3-4 different niches.** Start with one, execute it correctly, master your target audience, build your social media presence, and become successful within that one area before moving on to the next.

5. - **Don't be afraid to ask for help.** You're only one person, and you cannot do everything on your own. Hire a personal assistant. Have someone handle your admin tasks, someone to crunch numbers for you, whatever it may be. Build a team so that your business is growing and gaining at the same time.

6. - **Find a mentor or a business coach.** It's super important to learn as much as you can within your industry because you don't want to start doing something and then have to start over because you did it wrong. Work smarter not harder!

Of course, running your own business is never easy. My many hats include admin, designer, social media manager, and more on a daily basis. Needless to say, things can become a bit overwhelming. My entire mindset has always been one of balance, and that is one of the reasons that I maintain my day job while also growing Twenty One Design and Promotions. I found a regular job that I truly love working, and now I recycle the skills and resources learned from my primary job into my business. I also bring my skills and resources learned from my business and apply them to my 9-5. As someone committed to living in this dual professional world, I find that not only am I able to stay on top of my bills and finances, but I am able to save, do things that I want to do whenever I please, and best of all, I have great benefits that I don't have to fund on my own as a solo entrepreneur. I'm fortunate to have found a position with a company that doesn't micromanage me, offers a great deal of flexibility, and allows me to really bloom creatively in my own personal enterprise.

Speaking of balance, let's talk for a minute about Momprenuership. Baby! It's way harder than I thought. Once I had my son, I thought I would have so much down time to work on some personal things and my business… maybe even some client jobs as well. If only life were that simple. People asked all the standard questions: When was I going on leave from my business? Was I still going to work on my business after I have my baby? I took about a month off from my business after my son was born before diving headfirst back into work. Why didn't I take more "me time"? Well, because bills were still due, including food and a roof over our head. Our responsibilities don't stop because of things that happen in our personal lives.

Motherhood has easily been the biggest adjustment of my life. When I initially found out that I was pregnant, I immediately lost my mojo for being on top of things. From writing in my planner every week, staying organized, making sure I budgeted for my paydays… I pretty much fell off completely. However, I was determined to get things back in order after I gave birth. I had so many things planned during my maternity leave– I was going to do it all (I thought). In reality, I barely made a dent in that list. But I came to the realization that it's okay if I don't get it all done – things would still work out if I didn't somehow do it all. The important thing was that I needed to recover from pregnancy and from childbirth while learning how to figure out this thing called mommy-hood. This is one of the biggest lessons that I've learned in my motherhood and entrepreneurship journeys – to give myself grace and remember that it's okay if I don't get everything done. Work will still be there tomorrow. The important thing is not to burn myself out so that I can still be here tomorrow, too.

You always hear that moms don't get enough credit and honestly, WE don't. We do so much after a baby is brought into this world even in the first 24 hours after birth, never complaining, still tending to the house, cooking, all while taking care of the kids. It's amazing to me because we "multi-balance," not multi-task, multi-balance every single thing we have going on in our life.

There are always those moments that pop up quite frequently where I feel I should just throw in the towel on my businesses, but what I've built this far isn't something that I can just give up that easily. I want to be able to show my son what happens when you never give up and keep pushing through no matter what. It's easy to become overwhelmed when you sit back and think about all the things on your plate and what you have to complete. However, the reality is that all you really have to do is take a moment to breathe and consider these few key things:

- If you have the support system - ask for help!
- Refocus your mindset!
- Block off times in the day when you know you can work on the tasks that you have to complete.

- Be realistic with your goals and/or client's jobs you accept – you don't want to overwhelm yourself.
- Don't forget self-care. Don't be out here always working and forget about yourself or you'll burn out.
- Know that sometimes it's not always about the business. You may need a break to spend time with your kid(s) or family (that's when shutting down your business for a day or two can come in handy).
- DO NOT beat yourself up if you can't complete your tasks.

I suggest these key things because these are all the things that I know I need to work on to continue to balance my life as a working mompreneur. I can't see myself giving up on my business (my first baby), so why would I give up on my clients? I know they wouldn't give up on me, and without them I wouldn't have the business that I have now. Knowing it's going to take time, patience and consistency, but I'm here for the long haul. Things will fall into place as they should and I will just take it step by step, day by day.

I tell you this from the heart because I've lived it. I'm not perfect, and I've made plenty of mistakes along the way. I won't pretend to be the person to tell you what you should do with your own life. But I will say that whatever you do, know you have a sister from another mother who will support and uplift you in whatever your heart desires. Go for it. We can do anything we put our minds to.

Define Your *Legacy*

Katrina Caldwell

Katrina Caldwell is a commissioned notary public and loan signing agent hailing from Dallas, TX where she operates her mobile and online notary business, Admin Mobile. She is a mother, business owner, author, and community leader.

A dedicated public servant with a demonstrated desire to connect with and advocate for the community at large, Katrina founded her business on the foundation of her core principles: integrity, professionalism, and accountability. Katrina has held many government titles and focuses on protecting her community from fraud, identity theft, and poor planning for inevitable life events with services provided within her notary business.

Connect with Katrina:

Website: https://adminmobilenotary.com/about-admin-mobile/
Email: services@adminmobilenotary.com
Facebook: https://www.facebook.com/OFFICEONWHEELZ/
LinkedIn: https://www.linkedin.com/in/the-mobile-office/

Chapter Sixteen: Crafting My Table
Katrina Caldwell

Crabs in a Bucket - the act of being unsatisfied and content in a controlled environment, while simultaneously lacking the courage to move, but resenting the ones who progressively escape.

It's a harsh reality when you realize the amount of human "crabs" in close proximity to you. The discovery of the analogy led me to pursue a uniquely crafted freedom at full force like I couldn't have ever imagined.

I've always been known as a go-getter, even from a very early age. This did not change as I grew older and became a professional – in fact, I would say that I only became more determined to grow into my own as an adult. I recall days in my early 20s, fresh out of college, eagerly looking for new opportunities for myself. I entered into a career in law enforcement and built an impressive variety of skillsets as I worked my way up the ranks into positions including Deputy Sheriff, Detective, and Senior Sergeant Investigator. In less than a decade, I'd ascended into the upper echelons of my government unit, even earning a feature on CNN worldwide news through a viral video clip of me "just doing my job" at one point. From the outside looking in, it seemed that I had it all –

yet despite all of the "cool" titles and success I enjoyed, I still felt unfulfilled. I recall at one point a coworker, confused about why I didn't feel on top of the world with these new accolades, asked me, "Dang, what do you want to be, the President of the United States?"

It's difficult to explain, but I honestly felt like I just wasn't doing enough especially with the restraints of the justice system. In my last position in my 9-5 career, I worked in effort to overturn injustices by re-investing cases where people claimed innocence for heinous dna-based crimes. The justice system was just extremely slow – it was easy to become demoralized by the work I was doing every day. I found myself surrounded by miserable people who complained all the time, and I felt like I was shaving years off of my own life from the stress and frustration from the position. Here I was, young, valuable, with a sincere desire to help my community, yet I felt like I was wasting away. Law enforcement is ranked as one of the top careers known for suicide, largely due to these factors. As a mother, however, I knew that I had to make a strong effort to combat getting sucked into that space. I made an outcry for direction and guidance to deal with how I was feeling, but was told to keep my head down and try not to make too much "noise." I am a natural noise-maker and it was frowned upon to challenge and ask questions in the government sector. I was at one of my lowest points mentally and I recognized it. My mind, body, and spirit needed healing.

I knew at that point that it was time to begin developing my exit strategy. I immediately started looking for a way out, even though I felt untalented and not really "good" at anything. One day during my search, I ran across my now mentor, Bill Soroka, on YouTube. Bill explained how to successfully start a business with a notary commission. What? Even as ambitious and goal-oriented as I was, owning my own business had never been on the to-do list. Yet, the more I learned, the more intrigued I was by this idea. Maybe business ownership had never been explicitly in the plans for me but, it certainly seemed like a feasible exiting avenue.

Entrepreneurship Isn't Easy

While in my detective role, I was given my notary commission, but I had no idea at that time that I could make money with it. I'd always heard that owning your own business "isn't easy," but thought to myself, "Well, hell - neither is getting shot at on-duty." There was not one ounce of easy, wearing a gun and badge everyday as a Black woman. Nervous, but hopeful, I decided to take the leap! I had already started re-vamping my budget and trying to brace myself for the unknown. I turned in my two-week notice and literally stepped out on FAITH. I won't lie I didn't really have a "plan." But, I knew it was imperative for me to change my life not only for me but, my daughter. I told myself I was going to pull the trigger and if push came to shove, I always had that exceptional resume and my reputation. I convinced myself that all the tools I had in my intellectual toolbox combined with my fueling ambition was enough to push me through. Little did I know, I had begun building the foundations to my table. In September 2020, in the midst of the COVID-19 pandemic, I birthed Admin Mobile - a mobile and online notary office stationed in Dallas, TX offering a complete administrative service to businesses and consumers with legal documents. I also help families get their estate planning completed affording them a upper hand in planning a fruitful future for generations to follow.

Entrepreneurship forces you to tap back into your past and use previously learned work skills in your own business. All that project management you performed, having those executive assistant roles, etc. are all things you will use to be successful in your own space. This is your lifeline! Don't erase the knowledge you built while working for others.

Imposter Syndrome

After I developed all that courage to make my leap, I wanted to keep that long nice resume I mentioned earlier to myself. I was "worried" about people calling me crazy for leaving stability, dumb-lucky in yet another arena, or worse, a fraud. What did I know about owning or running a business? Nothing – however, just as with anything else, I am a sponge for learning. And so will you.

I had developed a strong case of imposter syndrome- a mental psych-out that causes high-achieving people to experience an inability to accept and acknowledge their accomplishments. I started a whole business! That is a major accomplishment and a legacy building tool. What should have been the most difficult thing was submitting my two-week notice. Instead, it was the inability for me to get out of my own way.

When starting a business, you will need a few pertinent things to be and feel successful: a positive mindset, a circle of supportive individuals, financial literacy, and a burning fire in you to never quit! You'll learn so much about yourself when you, "get out of your own way." You know how it's always been said "the sky is the limit" - you'll now feel it and believe it. You will start to surprise yourself with creativity. You absolutely must disable your thoughts of not being worthy. You are worthy! You've always been worthy. Never challenge that.

The Test of Time

When starting something new, researching, and building skill, you may start questioning your value because you haven't been doing it for 20+ years. Do not believe the thing in your mind that says you can't do this!

I experienced ageism for many years in my career. If you are young, you don't know anything they say. While this is absolutely not true, I know from experience that the thought itself can sometimes be crippling. Do not allow it to consume you. We all are lifetime learners. You have so much to bring to the table no matter what your age, socio-economic class, gender, or background. In business, other professionals and consumers don't care about any of the above. Can you do the job? And, can you do it correctly? Great! That's the whole concept.

In some areas of your career, you've been an expert but didn't even recognize it. Take the time to review your resume and the number of years you executed certain duties. Doesn't that make you an expert? Don't count yourself out!

Seize Every Opportunity

Early on in my business, I found myself quickly becoming more bold. This boldness carried over into my personal life as well. What prompted this change, you ask? I learned a very important lesson, and if you want to be successful, you'll learn it quickly as well: **You can only eat as much as you kill.** If you have no clients or are low-balling yourself by quoting below market fees to appease family, friends, and consumers, you are going to feel it (and quickly).

I've always been a bold person, but as a business owner I had to level-up. For example, one day I got a text message linking my name with a family member's home address, and inquiring about whether we would be interested in selling the property. The cop in me had lots of questions and immediately started a small investigation into this. The person on the other end was very open and transparent about where they retrieved their data.

I replied to the message," No, the home is not for sale," then made a small business pitch, letting them know that I own a mobile and online notary business and had the ability to make their closing process smooth and efficient. BOOM! I was quickly accelerated to the owner of this real estate investment group and became a team member for notary case management. This relationship has been very positive for me – they are hands down one of my favorite clients! Crazy right? The old saying," closed mouths don't get fed" is absolutely the truth. I don't know about you, but I'm definitely trying to eat (well)!

It's mandatory to be a billboard for your business. You must build the courage to consistently post on social media, even when you get 1,000 views but only 5 likes. (Trust me, people are watching the way you move, even if they never say it.) You have to tell people who you are, what you do, and why you do it. You must set-up automations and systems in your business to help deter burn-out. There is no room for fear in an entrepreneurial space. Seize every moment and opportunity without stepping on others to get to the top. You must have so much self confidence that you really do believe you can fly; and that Mary had a little lamb with no question mark behind it. Confidence is KEY!

Sis Gotta Go.

As you make moves and force yourself to grow, some people will steer away from you. You will experience life altering challenges and let me tell you, it's going to expose any phony people in your life for exactly what they are. For the most part, I have always had the "no new friends" motto. I learned in business, I needed to take that mindset right to the dumpster. Strangers I meet daily seem to be more family and friend-like than most people that have been in my life for years. Strangers are now long-lost favorite cousins to me!

On your journey, jealousy and envy will show its ugly head. When you begin to move differently, you'll notice that plenty of distractions will arise. You'll have to subconsciously develop tunnel vision in order to get where you need to be. You'll have to abandon relationships no longer suited for you involving family and friends, too.

You also need to learn how to initiate difficult conversations and develop strong conflict-resolution skills. The people who are for you will make themselves known (and those who aren't will too). Learn this early on: if they aren't for you, they gotta go! It's an imperative action if you want to live a lifestyle you've never had. Otherwise, you'll find yourself back(delete) in the bottom of that crab bucket.

Transparency moment: the friend I just described above? That was me, once - I am calling myself out on this. I had a few friends who decided to jump into the entrepreneurship space well before my personal light bulb went off. In contrast to the above advice about dismissing those who no longer serve you, it's also important to realize that sometimes people are ignorant on how to be there for you – even when they genuinely want to see you win. I never knew that liking my friends' business pages, sharing, or engaging in posts could help their digital algorithms rank higher on different social media platforms. So, I encourage you to invite your family and friends to your events. Tag them when you drop new products. Encourage them to share your posts. List "ways to support" on your social media channels. Many of the people who are in your corner may start to show-up more with some direction from you.

Asset Protection & Life Legacy

Admin Mobile's mission is to give intellectual, moral, and social instruction to various communities on how to be proactive against pain, developed from fear; poverty, from the lack of essentials; and poor planning, for the inevitable.

The only thing that is certain in life is death. While we are so focused on building an empire, we need to ensure we are protected if we are removed from the equation. And if not, what steps can we take to ensure that it survives us? In 2019, I lost one of my favorite aunts. In a year full of the most damaging hardships out of all my trips around the sun, this death was especially painful for me to process. What's worse is that, in planning for her funeral we realized just how unprepared we really were. There was no plan in place to assist in her transition, and no answers to any questions. All of my aunt's closest family members - everyone much older than me - simply shrugged their shoulders with exasperation. That experience buried a hole of disappointment and anguish in my heart, and became one of the building blocks on which I built my business.

From then on, I decided not only was it important to build my own legacy for my child and my future, but, to help others build and preserve their legacies too. We do better when we know better, properly plan, and prepare for the FORESEEN circumstances.

Now that everyone is on their own special routes to "getting the bag" (which is absolutely phenomenal), what "bag protection" plans are in place to sustain your assets?

Our first layer of "bag protection" should be LIFE INSURANCE. Many people fail to realize that having a policy is a tool for creating wealth for your family when you are no longer here and many other cultures are taking advantage of the benefit. No matter how much money you've earned on your 9-5 or in your business. Wills, healthcare, trust funds, retirement plans, and deferred compensation accounts are all articles of bulletproofing your assets.

I challenge every reader to make the time and funds to protect yourself and families by building beyond your current reach. Let's break generational curses of poverty and suffering, and start affording ourselves and those close to our hearts the opportunity to experience dreams as reality. Put some thought in how you'd like to leave your legacy.

As for me, I vow to continue executing Admin Mobile's mission statement, one day and one person at a time.

Deon Hall - Garriques

Deon Hall - Garriques is a speaker, an author, a certified holistic health & menopause coach and an expert in essential oils for women's hormones. She is also the proud founder and owner of Deon's Wellness Wagon, a wellness and nutrition coaching practice in New York. Deon has been featured in VoyageLA magazine and other local publications, and has been dubbed the "Menopause Mama" because of her success in helping menopausal women alleviate their symptoms and reclaim their bodies so they feel like themselves again. Deon has spoken at Fortune 500 corporations, wellness conferences, summits, retreats, community organizations, women's groups and on several health and wellness podcasts. Deon graduated from the Institute of Integrated Nutrition where she obtained a certification as a holistic health coach. Deon lives in New York with her husband, Richard and her two amazing sons, James and Jonathan.

Connect with Deon:

Website: www.DeonHall.com
Email: Deon@DeonHall.com
Instagram:
https://www.instagram.com/deonswellnesswagon/?hl=en
Facebook: https://www.facebook.com/deonwellness/

Chapter Seventeen:
A Legacy Built on Love
Deon Hall-Garriques

I was raised by my grandparents in a very small rural community in Manchester, Jamaica. Here, it seemed that entrepreneurship was a way of life. Several of my family members were small business owners. My grandparents owned a community grocery store, my dad had multiple businesses and my mom, while she worked a full time job, always had side hustles bringing in additional income. Coming from this background, I thought that it was only natural for me to also become a business owner when I grew up. However, my mom let me know early on that she had other plans for me. She wanted me to go to college and have a "traditional" career. Looking back now, it seems that she thought that path would afford me more stability throughout my life. Although I had no idea where I would go or what I would study, it seemed the decision had already been made - I would be going to college. However, even at an early age, entrepreneurship was my dream. So, I resolved to make my mom's plans work for me – I would go to college, launch a traditional career, and then use that as a catalyst for starting my own business.

After graduating from high school, I migrated to the United States of America (USA) to live with my closest aunt, Precious (Auntie P), and attend college. Auntie P and I had always been inseparable, and I was thrilled to have her to guide and mentor me as I navigated my way through life in this new country. One of the first challenges that I faced upon arriving in the US, was to decide on a college major. There were multitudes of majors to choose from and many were new to me. This was a major life decision, what if I made a bad choice? What would that mean for my future? There were so many questions swirling in my head, it felt like pandemonium in my brain and I was confused and overwhelmed.

As I had done many times before, I turned to my aunt, whose input I valued and respected because she has always provided me with sound advice. She advised me to choose accounting as a major. Her rationale was that it would provide a good career path, accountants are always in demand and it would allow me to achieve the financial freedom and independence that I desperately sought. My Auntie P laid out what I called a perfect career path with an accounting major: I would complete my degree, get a job with an accounting firm, take the Certified Public Accountant (CPA) examination and become certified, work for a few years to obtain work experience, and then start my accounting practice. That career roadmap was so clear, I accepted it without hesitation. Just like that, I was on my way to becoming an accountant with the ultimate goal of becoming a business owner. That roadmap remained with me for many years.

During college, I worked several minimum wage jobs and even got fired twice for requesting time off to study for final exams. While getting fired was devastating at the time, it was one of the best lessons I learned earlier in my life. The resounding message was that I needed to have more control over my life and my future, which meant having viable skills that would enable me to have more career options. Otherwise, I was subject to the limited opportunities available to everyone.

Shortly after, my entrepreneurial instincts led me to seek opportunities where I had more control over my time. I started selling Tupperware and cosmetics, and also started a housecleaning service. While these opportunities provided a good income and flexibility, it was difficult balancing them with studying.

The more I honed my skills, however, the more opportunities presented themselves to me. As an accounting major, I was introduced to the Volunteer Income Tax Assistant (VITA) program, where students helped low and moderate income residents prepare their tax returns for free. This was a great way to gain tax preparation training, a valuable skill that was in line with my future goals. It was also a rewarding experience to give back to my community - the gratitude that my clients expressed was priceless. Once I'd mastered the skills through this opportunity, I decided to utilize them in a different way. I launched a small but successful tax preparation service geared toward college students. It was not part of my aunt's career roadmap for me to start my accounting business this early in my career, but this opportunity made sense as it was a natural progression to my ultimate dream of becoming a business owner.

My 9 to 5 Journey

Upon graduation from undergrad, I felt ready to take on the world. I set my sights on working for one of the "Big 8", which were the most prestigious accounting firms at the time. Working for one of these firms would give me the experience I needed to start my own practice. My job search was in full gear; I combed the 'Help Wanted' section of the Sunday New York Times (before the internet) and after several months of pursuing the "Big 8" accounting firms, I was unsuccessful. I later learned that the "Big 8" only recruited candidates from certain schools and my alma mater was not on their list. I also learned about the ills of discrimination in corporations and the difficulties that women and people of color experienced when trying to climb the corporate ladder.

While this was very disappointing, I did not let it discourage me. I kept on moving in the direction of my dreams, but I needed some professional guidance to help me navigate my path. I joined networking groups and associations and found mentors who were willing to invest their time to offer me advice and guidance. Over the next 20 years, I found additional mentors and sponsors within my organizations who were instrumental in the trajectory and success of my career in the financial services industry. Although I did not start my accounting practice, my desires and dreams of becoming a business owner and moving beyond the 9 to 5 still loomed. The only difference was that my interests had changed along the way.

Early in my career, I was introduced to "Fit for Life," a health and nutrition book by Marilyn and Harvey Diamond. This book changed my life. It raised my awareness about nutrition and health and helped me to understand the REAL impact that nutrition and lifestyle had on a person's overall health. Over the next several years, I became a student of health and wellness, reading and studying related materials. I later became the informal health and wellness coach for my friends and family. My dreams now consisted of becoming a health and wellness practitioner instead of an accountant running my own firm. I needed to pivot from my well-laid roadmap and look into what lay beyond what I currently knew.

Finding My Niche Beyond the 9 to 5

In 1999 my Auntie P became ill and I started to spend more time with and helping to take care of my two cousins, who were both young. Within six months, she was diagnosed with stage four cancer and given six months to live, but thankfully, she lived for a year. I watched her rapidly decline to the point where she was beyond recognition. I sat by her bedside daily and talked to her or just watched her sleep. I felt like a fraud as my aunt was suffering and I had been studying and learning so much about health and wellness and yet I was helpless. I did not know how to help, I did not know if her condition was too far gone. I did not want to burden her with regiments and restricted nutrition protocol that I did not know would work. I would live with that guilt for years to come.

I also had a deep secret that I desperately wanted to share with my aunt - I was three months pregnant, and while I was happy, a part of me was sad knowing that my aunt would not be part of our lives much longer. I had to mentally prepare for that conversation. My heart would pound and my head would hurt just thinking about her reaction. I eventually told her, and we held each other and we cried for about an hour. There were no words, just tears and more tears and while it felt good to get it out, it was so painful, my heart was so heavy. After that day, every time I was with her, she would look at me and tears would come streaming down her face, and then I would start crying as well.

On May 23, 2000 at 10:50 PM, my son Jonathan was born and at 11PM that same night my aunt transitioned. I knew that she was waiting for Jonathan to come into the world before she left. Now my son's birthday means so much more to me than just the day he was born. My world was turned upside down and for many years I struggled to come to terms with my aunt's death. I lived with the guilt that I should have done more to help her. I wanted to turn these negative feelings into positive actions, but I did not know how or what to do. As these feelings continued to haunt me, it became clear that I needed to use my health and wellness knowledge to help women make their health a priority, make a big impact and honor my aunt since I could not help her.

The AHA! Moment

In 2013, I was watching Oprah, and a guest on her show was talking about finding your purpose and living your truth and not dying with your message inside of you. And I remembered hearing these words, IF NOT NOW WHEN? It was in that moment where I felt like I was overcome by a feeling, something moved inside me - it was the AHA! MOMENT that told me to get in action on this passion, this burning in my soul to make a difference in the world and help women make their health a priority.

Shortly after that experience, I enrolled in the Institute of Integrated Nutrition (IIN) and obtained a certification as a Holistic Health Coach. Before graduation from the program, I formed Deon's Wellness Wagon in 2014 and started coaching women on health and wellness. My practice later evolved based on my own struggles.

My Personal Struggle

During my 30's and 40's, I struggled with fatigue, insomnia, mood swings, hot flashes, night sweats and having just enough energy to get out of bed and get through my day, which affected my work. Additionally, I developed fibrocystic breast tissues and was deemed high risk for developing breast cancer. My doctors, including a Breast Specialist, Gynecologist, Primary Care and Radiologist stated that these symptoms were typical for women my age because of the hormonal changes. I asked my doctors what I could do to alleviate my symptoms and eliminate my breast cysts, but their answers were vague and provided no real solutions besides recommending that I continue monitoring the growth of my breast cysts and hope they do not become cancerous. My life was pure misery.

Since I had no answers, I decided to do my own research to find out exactly what was happening in my body. After spending countless hours researching and studying, what I discovered was life changing. I learned that I was suffering from hormonal imbalances and that there are natural ways to balance my hormones and alleviate and reduce my symptoms. This was profound! After making a few modifications to my diet, incorporated additional supplements, started to better manage my stress, and adopted a daily essential oil protocol. Within a couple of months, the results were strikingly noticeable. My energy increased, night sweats and hot flashes decreased and the cysts in my breast reduced. Using the same protocols and regiment that I used for my own healing, I developed a 5 Step Rebalance Program and started working with perimenopause and menopausal women who were having some of the same struggles that I had.

While I still work a 9 to 5, I have built a successful 5 to 9 wellness practice that allows me to do the work that I truly love, which lights up my soul, especially knowing that I am transforming the lives and health of women across the world. My practice continues to grow and evolve and I am so excited about the future and all the possibilities because there is so much more work to be done around women's health, and I have so much more to offer. My aunt's endless support, encouragement and leading by example was instrumental in me choosing accounting as my 9 to 5 and her death resulted in my building a women's wellness business in recognition of her legacy.

My business came to me through my own personal struggles – but this isn't necessarily the case for everyone. I encourage you to think about the impact that you want to have on the world – what difference will your work make on those around you? Use that as a starting point to finding and building your business.

Tips to getting more specific about who you help:

- Perform market research in your areas of interest. The results should indicate areas with the most need.

- Entrepreneurs often want to help clients solve all their problems because they have the expertise and think they can make a difference. While this may be true, you will find more success in choosing the one thing that you feel most passionate about and focus on that area.

- Pay attention to what others or your clients are saying about you. What do they say you are good at? This feedback could provide information on who you should be serving.

- Get to know yourself. What are your strengths? What can you brag about? What are some accomplishments that you are most proud of? What are you known for? Use these answers to help you narrow down your niche.

- If you have had a personal experience solving a problem that you think others may also be experiencing and could benefit from your solution, develop a program around that and make it part of your offering. That was my story.

Akiba Canady

Akiba Canady is an entrepreneur and community activist currently based in Huntsville, AL. Her career boasts more than a decade of experience supporting struggling and at-risk youth in leadership, academic, and mentoring pursuits. She currently operates Canady Creations, an online gift shop specializing in gift baskets, handmade jewelry, and custom-selected clothing items.

Connect with Akiba:

Website: https://canadycreations.com/
Facebook: https://www.facebook.com/Canadycreations/
LinkedIn: https://www.linkedin.com/in/akiba-canady-65506b152/

Chapter Eighteen: Breaking Cycles, Building Legacies
Akiba Canady

"Do the best you can until you know better. Then, when you know better, do better." – Maya Angelou

I was born and raised on the south side of Chicago, IL. I am the youngest of five children, so growing up, I saw more than I ever wanted to. Sandra, my mother has been my she-ro my entire life. Strong and capable, I recall watching her work long hours at multiple jobs to provide for my siblings and I. She would tell us that she was trying to "make a dollar out of fifteen cents," but more often than not, it wasn't enough. We remained below the poverty level for most of my childhood, and my mother spent more time outside of the home working than she did with the children she was trying so hard to sustain a household for. My mother wound up working herself to death, succumbing to illness at an early age after years of putting her health and well-being on the backburner in the name of survival. Heartbroken after her passing, I took a look at my own life, realizing that I was continuing many of the same patterns. I, too, found myself working multiple jobs and being absent from my children for extended hours as I worked to squeeze a dollar out of my fifteen cents. At some point, though, I realized that this cycle had to be broken. I realized that my children and I deserved better than poverty-level living, scraping and surviving, but never truly thriving. There had to be a better way out there.

Hustling and finding creative avenues for making ends meet has always come easy to me - this was something that has long been in my DNA. Babysitting, braiding hair, decorating homes, and cleaning businesses were all side hustles of mine over the years. This habit was born out of necessity - I needed help paying bills, purchasing groceries, and caring for my children who depended on me, so I had a hustle. And sure, I was employed – in fact, I was often working sixty or more hours a week at my "real job". But all the extra things my children needed weren't included in the budget of employment. I'm not talking purchasing Jordans or iPhones or any of those other fancy things that families more privileged than mine can indulge in. Those things were never even part of the discussion. No, I'm talking not being able to afford the birthday cakes, Christmas trees, or Easter baskets for my kids. Those smaller things that may not be "necessities", but they help make childhood normal and special for my children. As a mom – especially one who works as hard as I do – it was important to be able to give my kids a sense of normalcy. I never wanted them to feel like they were lacking. So, I figured out how to make it happen for them. If I couldn't afford certain things for them, I figured out how to make them instead. And sometimes life rewarded me with blessings along the way. For example, I made my children's Easter baskets every year for as long as I can remember. I wasn't doing it as a side-hustle at the time – I just wanted to make sure that my kids had something fun waiting for them on Easter morning. I had absolutely no idea, when I started doing baskets that it would lead to starting a business. In 2018, I started taking orders for Easter baskets, thinking I could branch out and make a little extra money on something I was already doing anyway. That year, I had 12 orders for Easter baskets. The next year, in 2019, I had 122 orders for Easter baskets. Talk about a blessing!

From Hustling to Business

"If something is important enough, or you believe something is important enough, even if you are scared, you will keep going." – Elon Musk

I believe in listening when God speaks, so the abundant blessing of orders was for me a clear message that it was time to start a legitimate business. In April 2019, Canady Creations, LLC was established. I was eager, excited, scared, and mostly inexperienced to the journey I chose to enter. I vowed to set goals and achieve one goal each month. When I first put all of my goals on paper, I found the list to be over 15 goals long! I decided that I needed to re-evaluate and choose specific areas to concentrate on.

I was also very disciplined in how I treated the income from my business. I was determined to treat this as a legitimate venture, instead of the usual side hustle, which made a huge difference in the way my business progressed. I was able to realize a good amount of success in a relatively short period of time because I didn't spend a dime of Canady Creations, LLC money on anything but Canady Creations, LLC. I didn't buy lunch, pay a utility bill, or even fill up the gas tank. Each dime I made, I invested in my business. I stayed focused on the goals not the profits.

This process was beneficial and rewarding. I was expanding with quality and quantity at a more rapid rate. Yes, I had bills due, but as I said before, I am no stranger to poverty. I can remember a time when my personal checking account was extremely low. I had just $23.00 until my next paycheck. Canady Creations, LLC's bank account, stated otherwise. I continue to pray for clarity and strength as I continued this journey as an entrepreneur. I stayed disciplined and focused on the bigger picture, and made that $23.00 work until the next payday came around.

I soon realized that my decision to start a business was just that: THE START. I discovered I needed to level-up my business acumen in order to continue growing my business. I worked on strengthening my problem-solving skills so that I could handle whatever problems came my way without needing to invest a ton of money in someone else handling the issues for me. I became comfortable with denial and strong in research and re-evaluating. I was denied a start-up loan, business credit, I was even denied a Payroll Protection Plan Loan when Covid-19 hit. I received more criticism then I received help and support. I soon discovered the meaning of expanding, marketing, overhead cost, customer service, selling, quarters, logos, slogans, branding, website ideas, settings, clear cut goals, investors, taxes, profit and loss, targeted audience, social media, advertising, models, employees, contractors, vendors, challenges, self-funding, and most importantly networking. All of this was an essential part of staying relevant and manifesting into a well-rounded business owner. I realized my lack of knowledge and how my comfort with poverty was crippling my business, because I was familiar with limits. Limits were unacceptable in this new phase of my life. I had spent years in hustling mode, but now I needed to be in business mode. Now was the time to educate myself and be teachable.

Ok, so let's get it, because I didn't come to play, I came to stay.

Don't Talk About It, BE About It

"The question isn't who is going to let me; it's who is going to stop me?" – Ayn Rand

My business struggles began when Covid-19 shut the world down. Now, with press conferences and statistics on the television twenty-four seven, fear began to blanket America. The stress of the unknown, the loss of jobs, including my own employment with major nonprofit where I was both COO and interim CEO (yes, at the same time) – it was all so much. Many teachers, nurses, and parents were overwhelmed with fear. People were afraid to even leave their front porches. The uncertainty of it all was overwhelming – everyone I saw needed to be uplifted, so that became my goal.

The early days of the pandemic saw a shift in the business model for many retail businesses. We as consumers were forced to order everything online from groceries, to clothing, to any other every day necessities. We were also working at home, and our computers and laptops became a prominent fixture of everyday life.

Many small businesses shut down at the same time the world did in 2020, unable to make the pivot to the "new normal". I spent many nights wide awake thinking how to overcome these obstacles and keep my own business' doors open. I prayed constantly for clarity and ways to stay relevant so that Canady Creations could survive. I knew I had to produce items that were wanted during the pandemic, and the world was overflowing with needs. The orders for my baskets had drastically declined between major holiday times, so I took the opportunity to revamp my offerings and make them more accessible year round. I decided to add earrings and ladies clothing to my catalogue to see how they would be received. In the beginning these offerings were nothing major - just a few sundresses to dip my toes in the market. Almost immediately I sold out of two types of sundresses, so then I ordered three different types to replenish my stock. I gave away a free pair of earrings for all online orders.

As I stated before, I am extremely familiar to hardships, poverty and heartbreak. So, I was not about to fold, give up, or crawl under any rock. I stayed encouraged, listened to God, and stayed focused. I joined groups that would be beneficial to my business. Women in business groups, entrepreneur groups, Black-owned business groups, marketing and sales groups… I joined them all in an effort to keep a pulse on what other entrepreneurs were doing as we navigated this crazy time together. I turned to social media even more, doing Facebook lives, participating in podcasts about my business, hosting raffles and giveaways, and participating in virtual events. I worked on my marketing and advertising, including learning to leverage the most impactful tool in my business: my customers' social media platforms and word of mouth. I recruited young females to model new inventory and post, post, share and post again.

Soon, my hard work began to pay off and the flood gates began to open. I was given my first big opportunity from Dr. Aisha Fields and Kundai Bajikikayi while at an entrepreneurship event. I was blessed to join Zenzele consignment, an African consignment shop in Huntsville, Alabama for my first brick and mortar opportunity. Today

Canady Creations continues to utilize consignment as part of my overall sales and marketing strategy.

I was also given an opportunity to join Mrs. Dee Dothard of Crimson White Boutique, an online boutique in Atlanta, GA, to sell my earrings in her monthly limited boxes. Mrs. Dothard was a huge inspiration and support system when needed. What's more, her subscription boxes were a major hit, selling out each month, and granting me access to more customers and networking.

To date, I have participated in over 100 pop-ups and other sales events throughout Alabama, Tennessee, and Georgia. I was folding tables and tents in my sleep, I did it so much!

My entrepreneur group held monthly events, which granted me the opportunity to network with hundreds of other entrepreneurs. I made it a point to participate in these events strategically, so that I could gain the most out of each opportunity. I purposely gravitated toward the entrepreneurs who were not still in the "figuring it out" phase of the process, but were instead well established in their respective areas and dedicated to flourishing, working hard and being transparent about their journeys along the way.

I've also invested in technology that helps move my business forward and makes me more accessible to clients. I danced around for hours the day I received the email from,

After Pay approving my application to have their payment plan added to my website, as a payment option. Slay Now, Pay Later - Interest Free. After Pay and the ability to offer my clients an option(s – I've now added Sezzle to my payment options for clients!) to pay for their Canady Creations purchases in four installments has elevated my business level significantly.

I'm now at a point in my business where I want to give back and invest in others who are on their own entrepreneurship journeys. I recently launched "Work Smarter Consulting, LLC" where I assist other new business owners in getting their business ideas off the ground. From vendors, slogans, emails, budgets, marketing, websites and more, I advise entrepreneurs on where to begin with their businesses and help them set their own monthly goals. I also continue to grow Canady Creations and am excited at the ways in which it continues to flourish. So far I have participated in four (soon to be five) fashion shows. I sponsor professional up and coming models (thank you to The Royal Umbrella in Huntsville AL), and all new inventory is posted on social media as well as my official website.

Staying true to the foundations of who I am while also being willing to learn as I grow has been critical to my success as a business owner. I continue to give a free pair of earrings with online orders, over one year later since making the transition to clothes and earrings during the pandemic. My email subscribers have grown from just 11 at the beginning of my journey to now totaling in the hundreds, and my list continues to grow every week.

My e-commence platform is Shopify. I am currently placed in the top twenty percentage in traffic from other stores that launched the same week on Shopify. The more traffic I receive, the more my items are wanted by others. I am now connected to Amazon as well, a monthly goal I put into place almost four months ago now, that I have finally achieved. I have an online sale every week, and you must be an email subscriber in order to get that insider notification (so please feel free to subscribe my website: Www.CanadyCreations.Com).

Canady Creations can be found at the NorthSide Flea Market every Saturday and Sunday in Huntsville, AL for the customers wanting to shop at a location. I continue to set and achieve monthly goals, and am proud of myself and my success - even if it takes longer than a month to accomplish. I am now fully self –employed, and I no longer depend on multiple jobs for my livelihood.

Thank God, Mama We Made It

"There is no limit to what we as women can accomplish." – Michelle Obama

I am the proud mother of five wonderful adult children - three biological (DeAndre, Sandra, and LaVeja) and two bonus blessings (twin sons, Tyler & Trent). I am a glam-mother of three grandbabies, DeLaney, Lydee and Loyal. We can afford to buy Easter baskets that now come from Canady Creations LLC, made with love. My oldest daughter, Sandra is following in my footsteps as an entrepreneur herself. At 26 years old, she is the owner of her own business - an online shoe store called High Stepping Shoetique (Www.HighSteppingShoetique.Com).

I can happily say that the cycle of working multiple jobs and remaining in poverty has been broken by my generation. The hard work remains, the dedication remains, the working long extended hours remains. The difference now, however, is that Canady Creations, LLC is the priority, not the 9 to 5. Now I'm able to build my own dreams instead of working hard in service to someone else's. Thank God, Mama we made it.

Jessica Cammack

Jessica Cammack, better known as The Mack Master, is a Gadsden, AL and a graduate of Faulkner University. Prior to becoming an entrepreneur, Jessica accomplished nearly two decades professional experience in the retail, banking, customer service, and insurance sectors.

In 2020, Jessica launched her business, The Mack Master Professional Organizing. Through this enterprise, Jessica supports her clients in conquering clutter and dysfunction in their lives, homes, and offices through the Power of Mastery. She loves being an advocate of change that catapults her clients to live beyond bad decisions, dysfunction, disease, life crisis, and limited time.

Jessica offers wide variety of in-person and virtual packages that unburden clients and allows them to have a low-maintenance life tailored to their preferences. She is offering readers of this book the opportunity for a FREE virtual space audit and discover ways to get more organized in your life, home, and office.

Connect with Jessica:

Website: www.themackmaster.com
Facebook: https://www.facebook.com/themackmaster
Instagram: https://www.instagram.com/themackmaster/

Chapter Nineteen: Mastering Freedom
Jessica Cammack

For nearly two decades, I nurtured and cared for their "babies" (or, companies) as if they were my own. Initially I committed to a career with hopes of being able to provide for my own little one, but quickly discovered that their merit systems would only ever afford me a 0 to 2% increase in pay, if any. As the cost of living and raising my little family increased, I found that my employee-satisfaction decreased. My pay was capped by "salary bands" and was honestly never enough to truly compensate me for my time and labor, nor for the quality of work that I produced.

I was increasingly unhappy and down-right confused at how I had gotten to this point. Was this the "American Dream" – the thing that we were taught from an early age that we should be striving toward? How was it that each company could expect me to loyally and dutifully work for them, while subjecting me to harsh and unreasonable standards? Like most "employees", I found myself being expected to work when sick, to miss out on important events for my daughter, to be both emotionally and physically unavailable to my family for long stretches of time, and even to forego my own well-being in service to their "job". After years and years of this kind of treatment, I decided that I could not go on living this way. I was feeling so overwhelmed and overworked that I almost broke. I had nothing left for my daughter or for myself, and I knew that this was not the life or the example that I wanted to create for her.

So, I decided to take a leave of absence to rest and get my priorities in order. During that leave, I spent time fasting, praying, and re-evaluating what I wanted my life to look like. I was able to gain clarity away from the demands of my day job, and in turn I discovered my life's purpose. With a renewed sense of vision and an understanding of where my path should be leading, I finally got the nerve to sever the ties with my employer. In the fall of 2020, I made the decision to quit that unfulfilling job and began a life of entrepreneurship. My mantra was "anyone can sign my paycheck, even if it was me."

While I am approaching my first entrepreneurial anniversary, I must be very transparent and explain that this journey hasn't been so easy. I'm not the ideal entrepreneur. I had no business plan, minimal funding, and no backup plan either. I was simply standing on a word from God. With coaching and His leading, I decided to channel my love of creating order from chaos and hung my shingle out as a Professional Organizer. I set my own schedule, consistently worked out, serviced my clients, and began living what I thought was finally a "well-balanced life."

I have dealt with the highs and lows of Ulcerative Colitis since 2001. Thankfully most of these two decades were spent in remission. However, this year that has not been the case. That ugly disease showed up and tried to show out! I spent March and April of 2021 stricken with pain and infirmity. I cried, prayed, danced, worshipped, fasted, and at times did absolutely nothing...

I have seen the hand of God move me from wondering if I would make it through to affirming my purpose and expiration of this sickness. I've emptied out and dealt with past trauma and beliefs that no longer serve me. I finally had a time to cater to **me**, to pray for **me**, to let God love on **me**, and to rebuild the trust and confidence in God that had been distorted from loved ones passing, bad relationships, ignorance, misunderstandings, and Corporate America burnout.

Thankfully, I come from the lineage of leaders, honorable women and men, who believe in leadership, community, and God's power. My father, the late Darrell "Mack" Cammack, was an inspiration to me while growing up. In fact, my business brand name, The Mack Master, originated very organically as a nod to my father and the lasting impact he has had on my life and the legacy that I want to build. Early on, he instilled the idea in my head that I would be successful in life one day, and encouraged me to use my innate talents to aid others in their own lives in whatever capacity that I could.

God has blown my mind literally and shifted my perspective to think more like my father. He has helped me clear the clutter in my mind and body that kept me stagnant and not fully living the mastered life e planned for me, my family, and my business. While I already serviced my organizing clients from a different approach, this year has prepared me to better serve my clients and those to come.

My leadership training, college course material, and the inopportune situations from those 9 to 5 positions are what now cultivate my business growth. Every program, system of procedures, and template I created in Corporate America help me stand out from other similar businesses in the marketplace. Contrary to what I'd always believed, those years spent working for others were not wasted. They made me relatable and relevant to the people that I want to impact, those who find themselves in the same position that I stayed in for so long – those who are assertive, innovative, hardworking, committed, and yet **thisclose** to burnout. Those people who are looking for, reaching for something more from their lives and their careers.

In the words of Napoleon Hill, the great American Author: "It is literally true that you can succeed best and quickest by helping others to succeed."

Becoming free from the daunting enslavement of Corporate America has yielded time for pauses and breaks. Quitting my 9 to 5 changed the trajectory of my thinking, lifestyle, and legacy. If I was still stuck clocking in and completing tasks, I wouldn't have been afforded the opportunity to actively coach my clients into overcoming bad decisions, dysfunction and disease, just like I did. This bounce back has afforded me the opportunity blossom into the lady I was never free to be, the example my now pre-teen needs to witness, and the Favorite Girlfriend that advocates transformational change and freedom to all those I come in contact with.

Pressing through entrepreneurship becomes more challenging as the demands for your business increases. To say that I'm just building is an understatement. One could proceed and say that I'm the example of generosity, grace, and poise. Overcoming lifetraps, mindsets, and statistics have been the highlight of my entrepreneurial freedom.

I eat, breath, and sleep mastery -

Mastery (noun): a distinctive state of being that encourages one to embrace inadequacies as he/she exudes faith, strength, and order in the midst of life's circumstances.

I'm learning as I go. And more importantly, from those lessons, I'm learning how to exercise my voice and my creative style just God's way. Leading from behind the shadow of an unethical, ignorant manager is definitely a pastime that will no longer rob me of my true potential. I was born to shine and must continue to actively participate in the creative work God is ever so graciously doing in me and my life. I've consciously chosen to heal after the trauma of what I call "doormat-ism." I refuse to be the good "yes girl." I now give things and people clear No's where necessary. I've found my tribe that reciprocates the energy I give. I am connected to stellar business friends that I now call family.

Becoming organized begins with decluttering the man in the mirror. I believe, and have witnessed, that as we deal with the clutter in our minds and hearts, mastering life becomes so much sweeter. I have learned that self-discipline is a must.

I am outliving the manifestation of my dreams and destiny. I no longer wrestle with who I am versus who they forced me to morph into. The never ending rat race is nonexistent to me at this point in my life. Instead, I am becoming a household name, better known as The Mack Master - Professional Organizer, Life Coach, and Favorite Girlfriend. Daily, I strive to be better than the woman I was before as I continue to lead the girlfriends I'm assigned to. I will continue service my clients with a spirit of excellence and effortlessly change lives, homes, and offices for the better, by the help of the Lord.

This is a reminder that you can be free too!

You can breathe, and choose to live life better!

You can clear the clutter and not allow bad decisions, dysfunction, and disease to rob you of purpose and joy!

You, too can learn to relinquish control and hire the right help to assist with ditching your 9 to 5 as you create the business of your dreams that enables you to live a mastered life.

So go ahead girlfriend. I dare you to break from the bondage of your 9 to 5! Write your story. Live your truths. As always, remember no one can support your dream better than you.

Cheers to your mastery!

Kiki Lazz-Onyenobi

Kiki Lazz-Onyenobi is a talented and seasoned Financial Advisor with a keen interest in helping clients meet their financial goals and secure their financial future, and a demonstrated history of working in the financial services industry. While skilled in Customer Relationship Management (CRM), Team Building, Spanish, Leadership, and Wealth Management, she prides herself on being a strong, persuasive professional with a Master of Arts (MA) focused in Development Economics and International Development from University of Nottingham, UK. Kiki has been honorably recognized by the International Society of Female Professionals for having shown excellence, perseverance and professional accomplishment, among other recognitions in service to her work. In her free time, Kiki describes herself as a great chef, avid reader, passionate mentor, enthusiastic singer, conscientious leader, and generous team player.

Connect with Kiki:

LinkedIn: https://www.linkedin.com/in/kiki-lazz-onyenobi-aams%C2%AE-2a1310119/
Facebook: https://www.facebook.com/Kiki-Lazz-Onyenobi-AAMS-Financial-Advisor-100174351995400
Email: kikilazzonyenobi@gmail.com

Chapter Twenty:
Preparing for the Harvest
Kiki Lazz – Onyenobi

Sometimes I think that there are three kinds of people out there in these streets: Those that are fated to be employees; those whose destiny is entrepreneurship; and the third kind….well…I will get into that later.

I knew early on that being in the financial services industry was in my future in some way, shape or form. It was not that I loved mathematics, and excelled at it, as the common misconception may dictate. I actually did well in it and thought it was ok. But that was not the driving factor, not for me. The feeling was strong because I was intrigued by the way "money moved". I found out just how much I enjoyed the sector when I got my first job after completing graduate school as a business banker with a major bank in the United Kingdom.

While it can be perceived as less popular nowadays, I went the traditional route – straight after high school, completed my undergraduate studies in Economics and then unto my graduate program in the same subject. My mother suggested a Ph.D. and I swiftly stopped her in that line of thinking. I am here for higher and further education, and I absolutely see the benefits to that. But I knew that it was not for me – not my ministry (at least not yet)! Thankfully, she did not push the subject. Of course, after the master's degree, the next step is usually to look for a graduate level job that will justify the LARGE portion of your life that you have spent in one educational institution or another by this time. I applied for the position, and I succeeded in getting it. I was one of the brightest interviewees in my group (their words, not mine) and was super proud when I got the call from the bank saying I'd been chosen. As a Business Manager no less! It was not quite the "sales director" role that I had told my grandad that I would be aiming for when I was a child. But I can imagine that even if it was, it would have felt just as great.

Thinking back on it now, I realize that I knew next to nothing about being a sales director....except that it sounded really good to me at the time!

At the point of writing this, I have worked in financial institutions over the years both in the States and in the UK. Role-wise, I have spent most of my time thus far as a business banker. The role has come with varying titles: Business Relationship Manager, Business Relationship Specialist, Local Business Manager, etc. In these positions, I oversaw portfolios of business owners, and managed those relationships. I was tasked with building and increasing my book of business with new accounts while nurturing my existing clients in growing their chosen ventures.

It was in performing my duties in these roles that I came to embody the THIRD kind of person I mentioned above – those whose role bears a resemblance to being an entrepreneur, but does not fall under that title in the strictest sense of the word. That is how the role was explained to me, and honestly speaking, that is how I saw it....and worked it.

My position carried a specialty in dealing with start-ups, those that are just setting out, or are in the first few years of business. As they grew past a certain revenue size, they graduated from my portfolio to that of my senior colleague's. And I gave a decent send off, like a proud mama. I am telling you, you really get quite protective of these accounts, especially ones you have seen grow from inception.

But that right there was the JOY of my role. The start-up stages of a business is such a precious time, even for a seasoned entrepreneur. There's the excitement of the new venture, the butterflies, the nerves, the preparations, the set up etc. These feelings are definitely magnified for those whose venture is either their first, and/or a product of a passion of theirs. And I got to witness all of that, before they potentially got jaded by some of the realities of the "business-owner life".

I liken it to pregnancy and giving birth in many ways. The beginning phase of the venture is like the "first trimester" – you have the idea, and you are mulling it over mentally. It is still new, and you may only tell one other person about it at this stage, usually your spouse, or a best friend. As the "second trimester" takes hold, you start to put pen to paper about what you are going to do and how you are going to do it. And just like a pregnancy, this is when you may start spreading the word about your new venture to a few people, maybe a family member or a few friends. And it is usually at this stage that some seek out a business manager for advice about HOW to start realizing themselves as a business owner, and what that would mean for them financially. During the third and final "trimester", as they prepare to "give birth" to this business, many of the things we discussed in that second phase now come to fruition, from the incorporation to attaining licenses, permits and certifications as is needed. For some this would entail the purchasing of equipment and inventory, similar to the idea of getting the "bigger" items ready for the baby, like the stroller and the crib.

Then they come through to see me, all paperwork in hand, ready to open their business account. The business is legitimized. The baby is born. It truly is a significant moment in the entrepreneur's journey.

I've always made a point of keeping in touch with my clients, and I did this for several reasons. Of course we were required to, at least once a year. But I went above and beyond that, especially with those clients with whom my relationship had progressed from me just being the "nice lady that helps us in the bank" to a friend AND client of theirs. This gave me the license and opportunity to develop my skillset in the area of relationship building, which has been key and served me very well in my career progression from that point. It was not only a strength of mine, but an area in which I excelled, and found immense enjoyment and value. So I majored in referrals, patronizing their businesses, organizing and inviting them to events that would be of value to them, and attending THEIRS in support.

I had the perfect training ground for my evolution into my current role as a Financial Advisor, in wealth management. So now I guide and advise on LIFE matters, skewed to the financials. The "gravity" of what I do has increased, and so has my determination in this space to do right by my clients. And yes, I still engage in many of the same practices where they are concerned.

As a member of the "third kind" club I can flex my entrepreneurial wings and dip my toe in the proverbial pool, without getting all the way wet. As I build my practice in this field, the many lessons that I learned, garnered and advised on from previous roles to do with finances and business are even more prevalent. And as a Black woman in this industry, I have learned even more. Laying all those lessons here is outside the scope of this piece, but I will leave you with a few pointers that helped me.

As cliché as it may sound, this is as REAL as it gets – PRAYER is KEY! I am a woman of faith. And even when I am not being the best example of that, God has ALWAYS come through for me – manifested in MANY ways - and for that I will be eternally grateful.

No man is an island. You have to build relationships. WHATEVER your calling or purpose. You may be an expert in your chosen venture, but you will be surprised at how much more you can do with the RIGHT people in your network. That has been my most valuable tool in building my empire, and that selfless nature I have seen exemplified in my connections inspires me to do better.

And of course, regardless of your venture, you MUST have a firm hand on your finances, or outsource that responsibility to an expert. Mismanagement in this area is one of the main reasons many businesses fail in the early years. Errors like underestimation of startup costs, insufficient working capital, bad cash flow management and forgetting YOUR own salary, are very common.

Just as one single seed can bring forth so much fruit, by sowing correctly, you will stand to reap so much more.

So invest in your dreams. Invest in your purpose. Invest in your relationships. Invest in YOURSELF.

Then smile.

Harvest is coming.

Acknowledgements

Kioshana LaCount Burrell (Editor, Publisher)

To my husband, Matthew - thank you for your enduring support and love throughout this and other journeys we've undertaken together – I love and appreciate you so much.

To my beautiful children – Matthias, Mattox, and Kaylin. Being your mom is one of the greatest gifts the world has ever blessed me with, and I so enjoy helping you along as I watch you grow. I hope to always be an inspiration to you, and to stand as a testament that success is more than possible when you work hard and believe in yourself and your dreams.

To Julian Long, who has worked tirelessly on helping me perfect this project. Thank you for caring about my work and believing in me as much as (or more than) I often believe in myself.

To Professor Charlie Hardy, Kwame Christian, and so many others who have given me useful, tangible advice over the years, helping to guide my path and shape me into the woman and boss that I am – I appreciate you.

And finally, to the beautiful women who comprise this book. Thank you for undertaking this journey with me. I admire the light that you bring into the world, and look forward to watching you continue to grow in the future.

Marci Bryant, MBA

Thank you to my parents, Wayne and Cynthia Bryant, for helping me to develop creative and technical passions at an early age, as well as giving me resources to monetize both skill sets. To Wayne Bryant II, for teaching me how to lead with love. To Mrs. Tanks for teaching me the importance of giving my best efforts in everything that I do. To Nakia and Jorell for inspiring me to be a better mother and woman every day. To my sisterfriends LaKeisha, ReeJade and Kiava for always believing in my greatness and supporting my dreams. To all the apprentices and interns who have trusted my expertise to help them elevate. To Mia and Leo for trusting me with your big dreams. To Jereshia, Liz, and Jordan for sharing your business brilliance. To Donna, Renee, Marilyn, Diane, Flora, and Rozina for always covering me with a mother's love.

Dee Burrowes

For every person who felt the dream was impossible. I am your voice, strength, safety net and support in your vulnerability. To my mother for raising me to believe anything is possible. I am profoundly grateful. Thanks be to God.

Katrina Caldwell

I'd like to thank God for affording me the opportunity to let my voice be heard and shared amongst this feminine cohort. Thank you to all of my mentors, family, friends and editor. I'd like to dedicate my excerpt to my beautiful daughter; Khari, my beloved, may you always have the courage to build beyond.

Akiba Canady

First, I want to thank God, the most high. The woman that has manifested now could never be without being highly favored and blessed beyond measure.

Second, I want to say thank you Kio for granting me with this wonderful opportunity of sisterhood. I am deeply appreciative and my inner worth went up to another level since you called me to take part in this project. You're a beautiful genius Mrs. Burrell.

Lastly, I want to thank my support system that consists of my world, my children and beautiful grands, who laugh at me daily but shower me with so much love and support.

To my big brothers, thank you for the life lessons. "Yes, It's greater later." To my nephews and wonderful cousins I want to say that I appreciate the support. That's love.

I like to say I don't do friends, I do sisters. To my entrepreneur sisters, you know who you are. I can't thank you enough ladies. The ladies who've been answering my calls for over 25 years, uplifting me and reminding me that I no longer have limits. You're irreplaceable. Kianeisha, Wanda, Monica, Debra and Lorraine. I love you all

Alysha M. Campbell

First and foremost, I would like to thank my Lord and Savior Jesus Christ, for which without Him nothing would be possible.

My chapter is dedicated to my incredible husband Nathan. You believed in me when I didn't believe in myself. Thank you for always being in my corner and for your everlasting support and love.

Thank you to all my friends and family that have influenced and shaped my life in so many amazing ways. I've never been alone in this journey and that is because of you.

To all that read this beautiful collection of stories, thank you. I hope it provides inspiration and hope for your path.

Lishala Carter

Thank you to my sister, DeAsia! You are indeed my best friend! Your love and support means more than you know!

Cassie Catrice

I dedicate my chapter to the coaches, therapist, mentors, leaders, and inspirational women and men who invited me to the table or have been a source of inspiration for me to believe in myself and walked alongside me as I create the unthinkable and believe the unimaginable yet certainly possible dreams (with God!).

I dedicate this book to God for revealing to me another way and mode of operation, for giving me a new perspective of myself, my health, my career, business, and my time.

To my niece and nephews, my future family, clients, future clients, and visionary women around the world. Know that you set the limits on what's possible, so aim high!!

To my mother who inspired my faith, the pastors / ministers (formal and informal) who covered my soul in prayer and teaching, as well as my spiritual mothers and sisters who held me up throughout the process. To my Father who has been an extension of God's love on earth by providing and protecting me. To my godmother, godfather who sowed early seeds in the journey and any person who played a role in being "the village" - Thank you.

Ristina Gooden

To my dad and mom – Reginald and Ronda – thank you for being models of radical hospitality and instilling in me that to whom much is given, much is required. May I add to the legacy that you all created.

To my best friends – Teneshia, Karlton, Quanta, and Pierrie – thank you for always showing up, holding space, and taking shots. It is an honor to do life with all of you.

To my mentor and friend, Mashaun – thank you for always seeing me and modeling the way. Because of you, I am.

To my niece and nephew, AJ and JJ – never forget that you are full of magic and so deeply loved.

Deon Hall

To my husband, Rich, for your love, encouragement and willingness to always support my endeavors.

To my children, Jonathan and James for being my cheerleaders, inspiring me to want to try and do new things and for your patience.

To my dearest Auntie P. (Precious) for your guidance, support and encouragement. Although you are no longer with us, you have forever changed my life and who I have become.

To my mother, Beverly, who insisted on me getting quality education at an early age, which changed the trajectory of my life.

Porché Maloney

To whom much is given much is required. Thank you, God, for the pressure to become polished.

Sending love and appreciation to my coaches & mentors: Syndra, Niaomi, YB, Kristen, & the Grindation community without your wisdom and influence the iron wouldn't be as sharp.

To my co-authors, I'm grateful we were able to share our stories and this experience together.

Lastly, thanks Mom for always encouraging me to make the most of life and for always saying "you should write a book" - love you.

Qiana Martin

Hey kiddo this one is for you. You make me always want to be a better person, but especially a better momma. God knew what he was doing when he gave me you. I thank the most high and all amazing working moms before me. You are appreciated.

Sheena Morgan

They say your ancestors leave lasting impressions on your life. Words spoken to you in your mother's womb or through dreams that seem to resonate in your mind in the most sentimental and reflective moments. It's those words of encouragement, empowerment, grit, and motivation that led me to the point of actual vulnerability and transparency.

Thank you to you, my family, friends, sister circle, and colleagues who have supported my journey.

Thank you to my mom, Vivian Kelly, and my dad, John Kelly that chose me to be a part of their family and shared with me a world of culture, vibrancy, and love.

Most earnestly to my dad, who ascended into the next world in 2013 but never stopped telling me how miraculously gifted I was. He lit the match that has flamed the fire of entrepreneurship in my life. His example of working a 9 to 5 and building his business that I reflect on most often.

Kiki Lazz - Onyenobi

To God be ALL the Glory.
Through HIM, all things are made NEW and POSSIBLE.
GREAT is His Faithfulness.

Keita Pyfrom

I'd like to thank God who is the head of my life and allowing me to be graced by an awesome opportunity. It is only through Him that all things are possible.

Thank you to my children who selflessly share me with my clients and have endured the struggles, but provide the most support when they can. When no one else supported my entrepreneurship, they were right there cheering me on. A special thanks to my mother who gives herself endlessly even when she is tired. I could not have accomplished what I have without her sacrifices.

I'd also like to thank my extended support system and my friends who were there for me.

Lastly, I want to dedicate my chapter to my father, who has passed on, but still lives in my heart each and every day.

Christon Stewart

Thank you to God, my son and all of my support system. Special thanks to the Thrifty Mama Media team for this opportunity.

Love this book? Don't forget to leave a review!

Every review matters, and it matters a *lot!*

***

Head over to Amazon or wherever you purchased this book to leave an honest review for us. We appreciate your time in reading this book, and hope that you received valuable, actionable advice to implement in your own business.

***

Good luck, sis – we are (still) rooting for you!

www.ingramcontent.com/pod-product-compliance
Lightning Source LLC
Chambersburg PA
CBHW031616210526
45464CB00004B/1607